MW01679852

13 BIGGEST MISTAKES THAT CAN DESTROY YOUR ARIZONA INJURY CASE

The Master Guide to Arizona Injury Claims

BREYER LAW OFFICES, P.C.
www.BreyerLaw.com
Alexis@BreyerLaw.com
Mark@BreyerLaw.com

Printed in the United States of America.

ISBN: 978-1-59571-348-3

Designed and published by

Printegrity LLC
283 South 640 West
Pleasant Grove , Utah 84062

www.print-integrity.com
1.801.785.8461

ACKNOWLEDGMENTS

A book would not be a book without thanking all of those who support you. We would like to thank both sets of parents for all of their support and love.

To my eight wonders who bring laughter and happiness to every day of my life:

Zev
Kailey
Tate
Ariella
Talia
Pierce
Karina
Cade

~ *Alexis Saphire Breyer* ~

To my co-author, wife, mother of my children, the love of my life. Without you this book would not have been written and the story of my life would never have been written nearly as well.

~ *Mark P. Breyer* ~

WARNING

This book will not make you a great and experienced trial lawyer. It will not make you an inexperienced trial lawyer. It will not make you a lawyer at all. In our first edition of the book, we were very happy to be providing information to actually allow people to understand a sometimes complicated and overwhelming legal process. We were happy to provide information for those people who could not get a lawyer to help them on their personal injury case because of the relatively small nature or size of their claim. However, we did not foresee the possibility that some may think that they have the ability to handle a serious personal injury matter on their own.

This book is intended to be a no nonsense, common sense explanation of the often overly complicated personal injury legal system. It should help anybody who reads it understand more about the legal process , which claims need an attorney, which claims may not need lawyer involvement, how to hire the best attorney, and what questions to ask throughout the entire process.

If you are seriously injured, you should not try to handle your claim on your own and should at the very least have a consultation with an attorney. Reading this book will no more prepare you to handle a serious personal injury matter on your own than reading a book written by Magic Johnson would prepare you to be point guard for the Los Angeles Lakers, or reading a book by Bill Gates would prepare you to run Microsoft, or reading a book by Albert Einstein would prepare you to explain and understand physics.

Of course, we are not claiming to be Magic, Gates, or Einstein, but our point is that one book – no matter how helpful - is not a substitute for the value of a top personal injury law firm.

Learn as much as you can, however, do not allow this book to fool you into believing that you have enough information to successfully handle a serious personal injury or wrongful death claim.

Enjoy the book!

TABLE OF CONTENTS

A Personal Message To Our Readers 18

Why This Book? 19

Who are Alexis and Mark Breyer? 21

This book is not legal advice (well, sort of) 23

Why Write This Book? 24

Our Current Legal System 26

The Honest Law-Abiding Citizen 27

Mistake #1
Failing to Recognize a Personal Injury Claim Exists 29

Requirement #1 31
Requirement #2 32
Requirement #3 35
Requirement #4 37

Automobile Collisions 39

Motorcycle Incidents 41

Trucking Incidents 44

Dog Bites 46

Construction Incidents 48

Product Liability 50

Slip and Fall/Trip and Fall Incidents 52

Requirement #1 56
Requirement #2 58
Requirement #3 60

Property Damage Claims Only 62

Loss of Use of Your Vehicle 66

Diminution in value of your vehicle 67

Mistake #2
Failing to Pursue an Injury Claim 69

Sometimes Bad Things Happen to Good People 71

A Lawsuit or Shotgun 73

Plaintiff's Personal Injury Lawyer 77

Mistake #3
Failing to Understand the Rules of the Game 80

No Smoke, No Fire 82

The Death of an Injury Victim 85

Going to Extremes: Laws that Favor Foreign Corps. 87

Ignorance of the Law is No Excuse 90

Ever Been to A Jury Trial? 92

Jurors that put a Price on Something 96

Suing the Other Party's Insurance Company 98

Expert Witness vs. Treating Doctor 100

Where the Law Allows Abusive Conduct to go
Undeterred, Expect Abuse to Occur 103

Mistake #4
Not Understanding "Case Value" 106

Waiting for a Complete Recovery 107

Mistake #5
Not Documenting Everything Possible
If it Isn't Written – it Didn't Happen 112

Mistake #6
Not Having Open and Honest Communication
With All Doctors and First Responders 120

Medical Records Twisted Beyond All Recognition 123

Opportunity to Get Justice Often Lies Within the Records 125

How One Sentence Can Force a Case to Trial 126

Mistake # 7
Assuming Lost Wages Will Automatically be Paid 129

Lost Future Earnings a.k.a Diminished Capacity 132

Mistake #8
Failing to Say "No" to a Request for a
Recorded Statement 134

Mistake #9
Filling Out Insurance Forms & Questionnaires 137

Mistake #10
Missing the Statute of Limitations 140

What You Don't Know Can Hurt You 143

Mistake #11
Not Being Aware of Lien holders Prior to Settlement 146

Medical and Other Provider Liens 146

Mistake #12
Failing to Consult with a Lawyer 150

At What Point Should One Look for a Lawyer 152

To Hire or Not Hire a Lawyer, that is the Question 153

Insurance Adjusters Have a Job to do 155

Mistake #13:
Failing to Hire the Right Lawyer 158

Ten Questions to Ask When Interviewing a Lawyer 158

Conclusion 165

PREFACE

It started like any other Wednesday. It was in late December, 2000. I had just met with a new client who had been referred to me by another Phoenix attorney. It was a mother, her name was Brett, who had lost her only child, Garrett, in a terrible and tragic car accident. He had been going through an intersection when he was T-boned. Not only was he the only child to his mother and father, but he left behind a loving wife, Gloria, and his 4-year-old son, Aaron. She had been informed that the other driver lived and said that he was not at fault for the accident. She wanted to know if we could help her. Not all of the time, but many times, when there is a liability dispute it's necessary to inspect the vehicle. In this particular case, it appeared from our conversation there was a probable claim that the seatbelt was defective and that was what caused Garrett's death.

I decided I would call the storage yard the vehicle was at so I could have my investigator go down and take pictures right away. Within moments of placing that call to the lot where the SUV was being secured, the next two days changed from ordinary to extraordinary, and our commitment to our clients would be put to the test. I called up and simply gave the vehicle identification and stated I just wanted quick confirmation that the car was still in its same spot, safe and secure. Instead, I was told that the car had been sold two weeks earlier. Thinking that there must be a mistake, I insisted that she double check, and then insisted she get a manger to make sure there was not a computer error. No, I was told after each attempt, there was no mistake. The SUV had been sold to a parts dealer. With no choice but to "find a way," there was no pouting or whining or wasted time. We jumped into "action" immediately to gather as much information as we could.

The only thing that we could learn immediately was that the car had been sold to a car dealer who had lots in Mexico. We were told that this particular dealer was a regular buyer at salvage yards in Arizona, and after he purchased the cars he would take the cars down to Mexico. Once in Mexico, the cars were torn apart and sold for parts or sold to whomever came to buy them. Once the car hit Mexico, the likelihood of recovering it was slim. In spite of the rapid-fire phone calls made by Alexis and me, we were told that it was a waste of time. The car was already in Mexico, and any effort to recover it was a waste of time.

So, here was the first real test of whether or not our belief that everything we've always said about our commitment to our client's case and our dedication to them, personally. At that moment, we could call the family, explain what others had done wrong, and simply wrap the case up. Here, with a car somewhere in Mexico and probably already long gone, the easy thing to do was to close the case and call it a day. What else could we do? We could sit in our office and make dozens of phone calls doing anything we can to track the car down but, when that ultimately and inevitably fails, have we really done everything possible?

Or, do we actually care? Are we actually willing to find some way, any way, to try to track down the SUV? The funny thing is, we never gave it any thought. The only option was to find a way or to at least leave no stone unturned. This was not a job I can hand off to somebody else. It was not something I could do sitting in my office. There was a car that was a vital piece of evidence that was the only hope for some kind of compensation against Ford – some feeling of justice mixed in with this overwhelming tragedy to a broken-hearted family – and there was no way I could do anything less than everything possible.

We spent the next 24 hours making every possible phone call to every possible person that might be able to track down the car dealer who purchased the car. We were ultimately able to locate, after who knows how many phone calls, the paperwork that demonstrated that the car had gone into Mexico a week earlier. From there, its whereabouts were unknown. We were also able to track down the location of one of the car lots that was owned by this particular car dealer. That's right, "one of the car lots" of this particular dealer. It turns out he had so many cars and so many lots that he was the biggest used-car and parts dealer in northern Mexico. However, nobody could tell us where the car was or whether it was even still in one piece. Valuable hours were ticking away, and we could not wait any longer. I had to get to Mexico myself. I had to be in the country searching around and doing whatever I could do.

Since I do not speak Spanish and certainly do not know my way around the streets of northern Mexico, I had to try to find somebody willing to leave the US for an unknown period of time who would act as an interpreter for me. In other words, I had to find somebody who could leave that night and drive with me to Mexico, try to find the car, and then try to get it back into the United States.

Now, in retrospect, trying to find someone willing to drop everything and drive to Mexico in the middle of the night to be there when the sun comes up is such a ridiculous long shot, and yet it was nowhere near as hard as the task ahead: head down to Mexico trying to find a car that may not even be able to be located by anyone, and even if it is found we would have to find a way to get the SUV back into the US. However, the car no longer had proper US paperwork, and we were told that the process of getting a badly damaged car into the United States that takes a minimum of four weeks. We had hours or days, not weeks. Somehow, we would have to try to make this happen.

The first step was to find an interpreter with free time. Through a former client, now friend, we tracked down somebody who actually was from the area of northern Mexico where we were going. I talked to him and we arranged to meet at a truck stop on the other side of Phoenix in the middle of the night. We had to be in Mexico when the gates opened to cross the border. I found my interpreter and we headed towards California and then south to the border. Walking across from the United States into Mexico would be much less memorable than the attempt to get back to the US. First, however, we had to try to find the SUV.

Sometimes, the harder you work the luckier you get. This is definitely one of those times. You see, as it turned out this interpreter had a cousin who was a lawyer in Mexico. The lawyer met us when we crossed the border and I spent the day with both of them as we tried to track down the SUV.

I will say this: I definitely saw parts of Mexico that day that most tourists never see. We went from car lot to car lot, from place to place, trying to find the vehicle. Meanwhile, during this entire trip, my wife and law partner Alexis was making phone call after phone call trying to track down the car. With the help of my tenacious bilingual wife, a lot of hard work, and a whole lot of luck, we finally found the car. I am not sure I have ever seen a car look as beautiful to me as the sight of that dusty, crushed SUV sitting in a lot in rural Mexico.

When I finally located the car, I still had a major problem: I did not own the car. How would I get the dealer to sell me the car and what would he charge? What do you think most people would do in this car dealer's situation? He knew I was a lawyer in desperate need of this evidence. He knew this evidence related to a wrongful death claim. He knew he owned the car and that he could charge me almost any price and I would have no choice but to pay it. Let's be honest, almost anybody would have taken advantage of that situation and the only question is to what degree. Here, once again, sometimes the harder you work the luckier you get.

Instead of taking advantage of the situation, the used car and parts dealer bent over backwards to be fair. He sold the car back at his cost of the sale and the paperwork. He did not even make a profit. And it is a good thing he didn't charge me what many would have. In my haste to get out of the Phoenix, I barely made it to the bank as they were closing. The safe was already closed, so the bank employees literally had to find whatever money was left in the drawers that had not yet been put away for the night. So, I left this small branch located inside a grocery store at closing time with thousands of dollars in small bills, including a large stack of $2 bills. I paid for the SUV, and now it was a matter of finding a way to get the broken down SUV across the border and back to a newer, safer storage facility.

We had traveled so far inside Mexico during that day that we were nowhere near the entrance into the United States that we had passed over early in the morning. With the help of the same parts dealer, we were able to secure a tow to the border. Of course, everybody in Mexico was telling us we were wasting our time. They were in the car business. They knew that you can't just take a crushed SUV with no valid paperwork across the border. Maybe they were right, but we did not come this far to quit.

When we approached the border, I was able to reach my Alexis and I learned that while I had been searching for the SUV, she had been fighting for a way to get it back to the U.S. in case we had found it. It turns out, Alexis had managed to get a hold of a customs agent and had somehow begged him into at least considering the possibility of allowing me to get the vehicle across. So, the tow truck dragged this car into the commercial lane for border crossing. Time was short. In a matter of minutes the border crossing was going to close for the night, and we would have to wait until morning - at least - if we did not get the SUV across in a matter of minutes. Everything hinged on these moments.

At that point, I asked for the borders agent that had spoken to Alexis. The agent said that vehicles that have no paperwork are not allowed into the United States. He went on to tell me that all of the customs paperwork and every other regulation would not allow this SUV to be pulled across. And then he told me about the conversations he had had with my wife. He told me about everything Alexis had explained to him about the importance of this family and the tragedy that they had suffered and that this was their last hope at finding some, small measure of justice within this tragedy. Then the agent told me that he was going to make an exception just this one time. I don't know what kind of charm my wife used to convince him to allow this SUV to cross the border.

I do not know why the agent was willing to do this. I can only imagine that he heard in Alexis' voice that she truly cared about these clients as people. I can only assume that he could see in my eyes the look of somebody who had not slept for two days and been taken all around northern Mexico at high speeds in a desperate search for people that deserved nothing but exceptional effort from their lawyer. I really believe that the US border agent saw in my eyes and heard in my wife's voice the fact that these two lawyers did not just say they would go the extra mile, they do not just say they care about their clients, they lived it.

We got the truck across the border but the Mexican tow-truck driver could not do anything more except leave us with the truck so we had to arrange for a Phoenix tow truck company to meet us at the border and bring the car to the new storage facility. We arranged for another car all the way back to Phoenix. Of course, when you have found a way to accomplish what we had accomplished up to that point, finding a tow truck to take the car hundreds of miles late in the day seems like a small hurdle to clear.

Years later - after we hired expert witnesses, took many depositions, and travelled around the country to litigate the case about the allegedly defective seat belt – Ford, the adverse driver and other parties settled the case for a confidential amount.

We truly believe we are different from all other law firms. Not just because we are a husband and wife law team, but that we don't just say we care about our clients, we live it.

A PERSONAL MESSAGE TO OUR READERS

This book was written as a resource for injury victims throughout the United States, in general. However, specific attention was paid to those injury victims in Arizona. While our commitment to excellent representation and service to our clients require us to be very selective in the cases we choose to accept, we still welcome phone calls and emails from anyone with questions. If you are a lawyer representing a personal injury plaintiff, or an injury victim yourself, please do not hesitate to call us. We are here to help.

We are open to answering any questions you have. We know this book is only the tip of the proverbial iceberg. In spite of our commitment to providing real answers and insights throughout the book, every case brings its own unique set of facts and challenges.

Whether you have a small injury or a serious one, even if we are not able to represent you in the matter, we will provide whatever guidance we can give.

Alexis & Mark Breyer
"The Husband & Wife Law Team"

WHY THIS BOOK?

We hope you will find that obtaining a copy of this book was a good decision. Whether you or someone you care about has a personal injury case, a potential personal injury case, or if you have always wondered how our legal system works, this book is for you. This book was written to give every personal injury victim valuable information about our complex legal system. Within this book, we have detailed many of the hurdles that injury victims must overcome to successfully receive compensation for a personal injury claim.

Before this book was written, there was no authoritative source an injury victim could consult to understand how personal injury claims work in Arizona. There have only been tidbits of information that were intended to aid the victim, arranged in difficult to find sources, that an injured person might find and, even then, only if they searched extensively.

Conversely, there has been a lot of information publicized by the insurance industry regarding personal injury claimants and personal injury claims. The information sent out by the insurance industry is often misleading or completely inaccurate. Moreover, the insurance industry does not provide information that can be relied upon or trusted by the injury victim. In fact, much of the rhetoric from the insurance industry focuses on "tort reform," a movement we view as often nothing more than a thinly veiled attempt at denying fair compensation to injury victims.

We believe this is the only book written with the specific goal of providing information to injury victims in Arizona, with the intent of helping to educate those in need about the legal road ahead. This book addresses how a personal injury claim proceeds, what roadblocks and obstacles are likely to be encountered, and what steps must be taken to receive fair compensation and overcome those obstacles. We address the reality of personal injury litigation in Arizona: jury verdicts are not based upon "facts," they are decided based upon "evidence."

Turning the truth into "evidence" that can be heard by a judge and jury are key steps in the process. Prevailing and achieving justice with an injury claim is not accomplished simply because the "facts" are supportive of the injury victim. It would be fantastic if justice was always done and facts were always proven. However, without taking the right steps and making the right choices along the way, justice will not prevail.

It is necessary to take certain actions so that fairness can be achieved. It is important to understand how our civil justice system works, and we have attempted to address that in some detail throughout this book. We believe it is empowering for the average citizen to learn why insurance companies and other corporate defendants act as they do when they are defendants in a personal injury lawsuit.

Lastly, we have highlighted some of the most common mistakes made in pursuing personal injury claims in Arizona. Mistakes that should be avoided whenever possible in order to increase the likelihood of a successful and fair result.

In writing this book, we hope to empower, enlighten, and educate. As the saying goes: **"knowledge is power."**

WHO ARE ALEXIS AND MARK BREYER?

We are Attorneys Alexis and Mark Breyer, "The Husband and Wife Law Team." We began our practice in 1996. From the start, we have focused our efforts on helping people who have suffered a personal injury as a result of someone else's negligence. We continue to help victims of all types of serious injury and wrongful death matters. Our cases include automobile accidents, trucking accidents, motorcycle accidents, slip-and-fall/trip-and fall incidents, nursing home abuse of residents, dog bites, construction accidents, medical malpractice, and other limited areas of negligence that cause injury to innocent people.

Mark is a "certified specialist" in Injury and Wrongful Death law. Less than 2% of all Arizona lawyers have earned this certification of expertise by the State Bar of Arizona. Only a small percentage of Arizona lawyers are even qualified to sit for the exam to earn this distinction. Among other qualifications, to earn this certification an attorney must have gone to trial for his client in a personal injury matter a requisite number of times as well as received positive feedback from other personal injury lawyers, insurance defense lawyers, and even the judges in front of whom the attorney has tried cases. After all of the feedback is received and reviewed by the State Bar, the attorney must pass a challenging exam which is given to test the attorney's knowledge and grasp of personal injury law.

After helping so many people who have suffered the effects of a serious, unexpected injury, we know that suffering a significant injury is traumatic. We wrote this book in the hope that the information we have written will benefit anybody who is going to embark on a personal injury claim, has already begun such a claim, or has a close friend or family member going through the process. Often times, it is the "unknown" that can cause the greatest stress and anxiety. While this book pulls no punches – we address in straightforward terms some of the obstacles that prevent a deserving, innocent injury victim from getting a fair recovery – it should also eliminate the stress of having no idea what comes next and how the process usually works.

Few people have enough understanding in these matters to feel at ease when they are facing a personal injury lawsuit, or even the fear of making a claim with an opposing insurance company. It is our goal to provide you with information to help you address a wide range of decisions, from the decision to hire the "right" lawyer for you, to the decision whether to even begin the process of receiving fair compensation.

While we are in practice together, it is not all that we do. Like most people, we stay very busy outside of our working lives, as well. We have a large family of 7 children, made up of 4 girls and 3 boys. While we have been lucky enough to never suffer the personal loss due to a serious injury, we have witnessed first hand just how devastating injuries can be to good, honest, fair people. Through the years, we have seen how another person's or company's reckless choices can change the life of the average person in the blink of an eye. This book will provide some measure of comfort to those who are facing the legal challenges ahead of them by providing some of the most valuable assets a lawyer can give: knowledge, honesty, and answers.

THIS BOOK IS NOT LEGAL ADVICE (WELL, SORT OF)

OK, almost every book has a disclaimer, so this one is ours. This legal book that provides legal information on a legal topic written by lawyers with experiences and credentials in the area of the law is not legal advice!

Now, let us explain what we mean. We stand behind everything that we have written in this book. However, though it may sound cliché, every case is different. Every specific set of facts calls for a different analysis. The number of factors and "moving parts" that make up the sum of a potential personal injury case are seemingly endless. Changing even one small factor can change the case strategy entirely. Changing even a little bit of evidence can change a case from a legal standpoint. In addition, the laws are constantly changing.

As a result, you should not make decisions on a specific case based upon this book.

WHY WRITE THIS BOOK?

"We the jury, duly empanelled and sworn, upon our oath do find in favor of the defendant."

These are the words read in court when a jury returns a verdict completely in favor of a defendant, awarding nothing to the plaintiff. These words are extremely difficult to hear when you are a plaintiff in a personal injury trial. To the personal injury plaintiff – to that good, decent person whose life was already altered by the injury they have suffered - these words must feel like a body blow from the heavyweight champion of the world. These words – a jury verdict for the defense – have ramifications far beyond the day they are read.

A jury verdict in favor of the defendant in a personal injury case can devastate lives and deny justice to innocent victims. What the average American may not know is that there are verdicts on behalf of defendants every day. While some of those verdicts are justified by the evidence, there are "defense verdicts" that are the result of bad laws, poor evidence, or failed planning.

As lawyers, we are armed with knowledge. We saw a need to share our knowledge and experience with others. We wanted to give injury victims a source to rely upon to better educate them in a legal arena that they may unwillingly became a part of due to someone else's negligence. Regardless of whether a case merits hiring an attorney - which we will discuss later, it is important to understand the way the legal system is set up, and how personal injury cases work their way through the system.

This book details much of the critical information an injury victim or his/her family need to know. Even if you do not have an injury claim, this book contains valuable information for you regarding our jury system and the insurance industry, and their combined effects on personal injury claims.

OUR CURRENT LEGAL SYSTEM

There are times when, due to our frustration with the hurdles that are placed in front of deserving people, we voice disgust at rulings, laws, and verdicts that favor defendants in personal injury cases. However, we strongly believe that an innocent defendant should prevail. A false claim of injury or exaggerated claim by an alleged injury victim should be rejected. We are in favor of justice in the legal system. In our view, however, justice is often denied to the person who was injured and to whom fair compensation should be awarded under the law.

A defense verdict for a seriously injured Plaintiff, who is an innocent victim of the recklessness of another, is neither justifiable nor fair. Unfortunately, our current legal system often rewards the negligent party and punishes the injured victim. We hope to help injured parties avoid making crucial mistakes in pursuing their injury claim so that if their case goes to trial, they hear:

"We the jury duly empanelled and sworn, upon our oath do find in favor of the Plaintiff."

THE HONEST, LAW-ABIDING CITIZEN

More often than not, it is the most honorable, sincere, compassionate, law-abiding citizens that find themselves being denied justice by our current legal system in personal injury cases. Why? It is because usually it is the honest, trusting citizens that wait the longest to consult with an attorney. These are the people who do everything that the insurance adjuster working on behalf of the at-fault defendant asks of them, not realizing that their trust is misplaced. They often start with no intention of even considering hiring a lawyer or filing a lawsuit, and they often suffer greatly as a result of this otherwise admirable mind set.

If victims knew how our legal system worked and understood the process of pursuing an injury claim, these well-intentioned victims could increase their likelihood of a fair settlement or favorable jury verdict. If people were simply provided valuable information and warned of the potential pitfalls, they are more likely to increase the chances of a just result for their injury claim.

We know, from our many jury trials and successful settlements for our clients that a fair jury verdict in favor of the injury victim can provide needed medical bills, reimbursement of money from a job that can never be performed again, and an overall return to something approaching the quality of life experienced before the injury. A jury verdict for the plaintiff, in particular, is something that announces that the injury victim – our client – has overcome all of the hurdles and built-in impediments to recovery, survived all of the challenges, and come out with a fair result.

Are you ready to learn some of what you need to know about personal injury claims? By the end of this book, you should be able to make an informed decision about what steps you need to take for you or your loved ones if they are ever faced with filing a personal injury claim. You should also understand the mistakes and pitfalls that must be avoided in pursuing such a claim.

So, let's get to it!

MISTAKE #1

FAILING TO RECOGNIZE A PERSONAL INJURY CLAIM EXISTS

There are many types of injuries that are suffered as a result of someone else's negligence. However, not every injury is meant to be compensated under the law. In fact, although we have no statistics on the subject, it is probable that most injuries are not compensable under the law.

Regardless of the type of case, most personal injury cases have specific requirements that must be met under the law in order to have the opportunity to obtain compensation for the injury victim. What evidence is required under the law to meet these criteria can vary widely depending on the type of personal injury case, but these different considerations must always be taken into account. These requirements that are incumbent upon any personal injury plaintiff to prove include:

1) prove a person/party was negligent and responsible for the incident;

2) prove that the negligence/incident caused an injury;

3) prove the extent and duration of the injury and any damages that arose as a result; and

4) be able to obtain the money owed from the responsible party/parties

As each of these elements are vital to the ability to pursue a personal injury claim, they are each addressed individually, below. Although these criteria are each distinct and necessary elements of an injury claim, remember that this is not a situation where "most" is good enough. Either all four requirements must be met or no recovery is likely to occur.

REQUIREMENT #1

PROVE A PERSON/PARTY WAS NEGLIGENT AND RESPONSIBLE FOR THE INCIDENT

A personal injury claim only exists when someone other than the injured person recklessly or negligently causes an injury to the victim. For instance, over the years we have talked to people who wanted to know if they could make a claim where they were injured in an accident that they, themselves, caused. By way of example, one mother called us after her daughter negligently drove into the rear end of another vehicle. The mother wanted to know if her daughter could make a claim through her insurance policy as a result of the medical bills incurred by her daughter.

We explained that it is possible that the daughter may be able to receive reimbursement of her medical bills from their own insurance company, depending on which insurance coverage had been purchased prior to the incident. However, the first step in a personal injury claim begins with being able to prove that another person was negligent. Well, in this example there was someone that was negligent: the mother's own daughter. An injury victim that was the cause of her own injuries has no personal injury claim. Since no one else caused the injury, the potential "case" would not make it past this first requirement in the analysis.

REQUIREMENT #2

PROVE THAT THE NEGLIGENCE/INCIDENT CAUSED AN INJURY

Fortunately, most negligent acts do not result in an injury. It is also fortunate that even where an injury occurs to an innocent person, and even where that injury was caused by someone else's neglect, the injury is often minimal. Most injuries that are inconsequential are not worthy of bringing a personal injury claim.

To have a valid personal injury claim, it is not enough that a negligent act caused an injury. Instead, the victim must be able to *prove* that he/she suffered an injury as a result of another's negligence. While the allegation of a new injury (or aggravation of prior injury) must be true, it must also be able to be proven with evidence.

We frequently get calls from people that were involved in an incident caused by the negligence of someone else. Though these individuals were not injured, they are understandably angry that their lives were impacted by another's carelessness or, sometimes, outright recklessness. We are asked by these people whether they can bring a personal injury claim. The answer is no.

Of course, to whatever degree their lives were impacted by the event, they have a theoretical right to make a claim. The defendant or insurance company for the defendant may be willing to offer a small settlement in order to close the claim to eliminate financial exposure for a belated injury claim. However, to have a personal injury case one must be able to prove an injury resulting from the initial incident. If someone cannot prove they suffered an injury, they have not met this necessary element of a personal injury claim.

This type of question from someone who was not injured in an incident most often takes the form of someone who was involved in a car accident. The people who raise this question are usually relieved that they were among the lucky ones who were not hurt. However, they may need their car repaired, or need a rental car, or have a need to get the car declared a total loss so they can purchase a new car. Of course, the law does provide protection to someone with car damage or any type of property damage, due to another person's negligence; however, this is not really a "personal injury" action, but a "property damage" claim.

The insurance industry – both in the insurance policies they write and in the way they process the claims – usually treat property damage separate from an injury claim. Anything related to a rental car, items damaged in a car at the time of an incident, loss of value to a vehicle, and so forth often are handled as distinct claims from an injury claim.

From a practical standpoint, it is usually lawyers that handle personal injury claims that also take care of these property damage claims for their clients. The legal issues are similar, the factual issues are similar, and it simply makes the most sense for one law firm to handle these issues for their clients.

We discuss the different elements of property damage claims later in this book. Since so many people with personal injuries resulting from a car accident also have property damage claims, we felt it would be a benefit to our readers to provide this information regarding property damage claims.

However, it is important to understand this distinction between a personal injury claim and the related property damage claim: if no injury can be proven, no "personal injury" action exists.

REQUIREMENT #3

PROVE THE EXTENT AND DURATION OF THE INJURY AND ANY DAMAGES THAT AROSE AS A RESULT

Proving the extent and duration of an injury can be the most complex part of a personal injury claim. Often times, the biggest effect an injury has on a person is the physical limitation caused by the pain they experience.

As personal injury lawyers, we have grown to hate the words "pain and suffering" because this phrase has come to have a negative connotation to describe a person who has filed an injury claim as a money-hungry, lawsuit happy plaintiff. Yet pain is often very real and can be devastating to the injured person.

What is difficult in proving an injury claim is that pain cannot be seen, cannot be heard, and cannot be measured. Two people can have identical injuries, but one person is able to still work and live their life, while the other person remains bedridden. Whether this differing result from the same injury is due to pain tolerance, luck, determination, or exaggeration varies tremendously. Yet, somehow, a personal injury plaintiff must prove that his/her loss of enjoyment of life is the result of the injury, not a lack of determination to get better or, far worse, a desire to use a lawsuit to get money that is undeserved.

In addition to proving the extent of the injury, the duration of the injury must be proven. In other words, it is our job to prove how long an injury will last and what affect it will have on our client's life. This is more difficult when you consider the trial of every client's case is a one-time event. There is no mechanism in our system of justice to return in the future and see how the victim is handling the injury years later. Thus, we must prove something that cannot be known with certainty: the future. We "prove" the future outcomes for our clients by comparing them to others who have previously suffered similar injuries and examining medical documentation. If you think this can often be difficult, and sounds like an inexact science, you are correct.

REQUIREMENT #4

BE ABLE TO OBTAIN THE MONEY OWED FROM THE RESPONSIBLE PARTY/PARTIES

This "fourth part" of a personal injury case is not written anywhere in the law. It is not in any textbooks we read in law school, and it is rarely covered in any of our personal injury conferences. It is not usually covered in the conferences where we have spoken to other lawyers, nor in the conference we have attended. However, this requirement is often as important to the injured person as the first three elements. Someone can prove they were badly injured due to the negligent actions of another, prove they were seriously hurt, and prove the extent of those injuries. They can receive a fair and just verdict awarding reasonable damages to compensate them for the effect the incident had on their life. The judge can sign the final paperwork, which is called a judgment, and make the verdict official.

The injury victim now has a signed judgment awarding them money against the at-fault defendant. It is now a matter of law that the defendant must pay every penny of this judgment. Now, what? Well, if that defendant has no money and no assets, that judgment is not worth the paper it is printed on. The phrase "you can't get blood from a turnip" often comes to mind. Basically, the fourth element that we discuss with our potential clients is the need to be able to ensure that a judgment against the at-fault defendant will result in actual benefit to a victim. Otherwise, the entire claim and litigation process – the time, effort, and energy invested by the client and his lawyers is a waste.

THE MANY DIFFERENT TYPES OF PERSONAL INJURY CASES

Attempting to list every possible type of personal injury claim would be nearly impossible. In fact, usually when someone's negligence causes injury to another, there is a potential personal injury claim. Over the years, we have learned that the failure to use common sense or due care can cause injuries in an untold number of ways. If a lawyer spends as much time helping injury victims as we have, at some point it feels like there is no completely safe activity; no human endeavor that does not rely upon the careful efforts of someone else.

We have seen a wide variety of unexpected causes of injury. These unusual or atypical cases have included a cabinet not properly anchored in the wall falling on an elderly woman doing her laundry; a go-cart causing third degree burns during a single ride around the track; a front-wheel of a bike coming off during a father's ride with his son; an improperly wired light switch causing severe electric shock, and many others. We have helped so many people following injuries we know that, unfortunately, there is always something new, something different, some other way that the reckless conduct of one person can lead to life-altering injury to someone else.

Nonetheless, there are some typical ways in which injuries occur. These more common causes of injuries account for the vast majority of personal injury cases and will be discussed below.

AUTOMOBILE COLLISIONS

Automobile collisions are the most common type of personal injury claims. The high rate of personal injury claims arising from automobile crashes likely results from the vast amount of time we Americans spend in our vehicles. We rely on our cars and trucks, making it easy to ignore the inherent risk of traveling at 65 miles-per-hour while sharing the road with anyone old enough to get a driver's license. We have all had the experience of watching someone drive who, by the way the car is being maneuvered, does not seem capable of walking and chewing gum at the same time.

Meanwhile, as a society, we trust almost every adult to get behind the wheel of a two-ton vehicle which is traveling at 100 feet per second, while eating a hamburger, changing the radio station and – all too often – talking on the cell phone.

Even under perfect conditions - with a conscientious driver paying attention to the road - we still have vehicles traveling at high speeds with inevitable human error. Thus, it is not a surprise that the most common type of personal injury claim arises from auto accidents.

Perhaps because it is the most common cause of injury, analyzing the personal injury case does not require any extra steps when an injury arises from an automobile incident than the four requirements we have outlined above. Of course, there are many different nuances to automobile collision cases that must be dissected on a case by case basis. As you will see in the sections that follow, other types of personal injury cases merit additional analysis or consideration beyond the four requirements we have outlined above. These claims would include motorcycle, dog bite, and premise liability cases, more commonly known as slip and falls.

MOTORCYCLE INCIDENTS

Motorcycle cases come with an additional set of issues that do not exist in many car or truck crashes. First, there is a predisposition of many people in the country to question the motorcycle rider or immediately assume it is the rider's fault. Regardless of the many possible explanations for this bias, it is a factual issue that must be overcome, even when the law supports the motorcyclist.

Second, motorcycle incidents are often extremely serious. The data backs this up. In 2006, 4,810 motorcycle riders were killed in the United States. As high of a number as this is, it does not even touch upon the approximately 88,000 motorcyclists that were injured - often very seriously - in 2006. Unfortunately, these numbers are growing. According to the results of this data compiled by the National Highway Traffic Safety Association ("NHTSA"), the number of fatalities for motorcyclists has risen every year since 1997.

Most striking of all, according to the 2006 NHTSA report, a motorcyclist is 37 times more likely to die in a crash, per mile driven, than someone riding in a car. Does this mean it is the motorcyclist's fault more often? Of course, not. However, these numbers do tell a story of the serious risks involved if a motorcyclist has a crash. Unfortunately, a "fender bender" for a vehicle is often far worse when the person who is struck is on a motorcycle.

Third, every state has different helmet laws and those laws are applied differently depending on the jurisdiction. Understanding those laws is vital, both from a legal and factual standpoint. For instance, the NHSTA data tells us that a motorcycle rider is 40% more likely to be killed if not wearing a helmet. Beyond those numbers, the law can be unforgiving. Many states require helmet usage while other states do not have this requirement.

While Arizona is one of the states that does not require riders to wear a helmet while riding a motorcycle, it will allow juries to be told of the rider's failure to wear a helmet if an injury occurs. There is a necessary legal analysis that must take place to determine if this information will be told to the jury, including the availability of a helmet to the injury victim as well as the evidence that demonstrates - or fails to demonstrate - the increased injury caused by the failure to wear a helmet.

This strikes many Arizona motorcyclists as completely unfair. If the law does not require helmet use, how can the failure to wear a helmet be introduced as evidence and used against the injured victim? Unfortunately, there are certain motorcycle accidents that, under Arizona law, allow the lack of helmet use to be presented to a jury. One key when pursuing an injury claim after a motorcycle accident is to remember that it is not necessarily a matter of what is "fair" but, instead, a question of what a victim must do to adequately protect him/herself from an insurance company's tactic of blaming the victim for not wearing a helmet that was not even required by law.

Having conducted and participated in jury research, we know that many people will blame the victim for failing to wear a helmet, even if that helmet was of little or no value of protecting the motorcyclist. Understanding how to focus the judge and jury on the at-fault driver instead of the lack of a helmet, as well as staying abreast of the changing laws related to motorcycle helmet use and admissibility in court, is vital to the motorcycle injury victim.

TRUCKING INCIDENTS

The world has changed dramatically in the last 15 years, and the effect of these changes have had a dramatic effect on trucking/tractor-trailer cases. There are federal guidelines that limit the amount of hours a trucker can drive. These are not random government regulations intended to limit a driver's income, but rather these regulations are meant to help decrease driver fatigue. Truck driver fatigue is one of the major causes of truck crashes and fatalities.

The federal regulations state in part that truck drivers are limited to driving a maximum of 11 hours after 10 consecutive hours off duty. A truck driver may not drive or work beyond the 14th hour after coming on duty, following 10 consecutive hours off-duty. Finally, a trucker may not drive after 70 hours on duty in 8 consecutive days. A driver may restart an 8 day consecutive period only after taking 34 or more consecutive hours off duty.

The violation of these rules is often the cause of horrendous collisions. It is easy to understand why truck drivers choose to exceed these hours as they are usually paid by the mile. It also is not a surprise that the companies that employ these drivers will often choose to look away - or even encourage - these drivers to exceed the limits, in the pursuit of greater profits.

In the old days, it was more difficult to prove that a truck driver was over his hours as a second, fraudulent set of log books could make it appear that the trucker was under-hours. With technology, however, lawyers have more methods to utilize in proving that a trucker was over hours and that fatigue was a cause of the collision. Today, almost every truck on the highway has an Electronic Control Module inside of it. This module is more commonly known as a black box. This unit electronically gathers data of how fast a vehicle was travelling, how much braking was done prior to the incident, and other factors that can provide valuable evidence of driver input or fatigue.

Also, most trucks are now monitored by QualComm or similar electronics that track where a truck has been and can help determine the amount of driving that has been done. There are other companies that electronically gather the fuel purchases to help determine how far the truck has travelled. Knowing how to make sure that the black box and other key evidence is preserved, and not destroyed, can be vital following some trucking accidents.

DOG BITES

Dogs are absolutely fantastic family members/pets for many of us. However, failure to keep the family pet in a safe and secure area leads, on far too many occasions, to dog bites. Sometimes a dog bite is not very serious. When we receive calls on dog bites, however, it is often because the dog inflicted a terrible injury. Making matters worse, the victim is often a child.

The laws that govern dog bites vary from state to state. In Arizona, there are two separate sets of laws that can provide a personal injury claim to a dog bite victim. Knowing which law to utilize - and more importantly when to initiate the lawsuit to keep the more favorable law available - is a necessity.

Unlike many states, Arizona does not allow for "one free bite" when it comes to the responsibility of the dog owner to protect others. In a traditional case, people are only liable for their negligence. In other words, people are not liable to other people simply because there was an injury. In most cases, someone is not held responsible if an injury occurred that was not foreseeable.

When it comes to dog bites in Arizona, there is a statute that changes that to some degree. Under Arizona law regarding dog bites, the dog owner is usually responsible even if it is the first time the dog bit anyone and even if the dog never showed any signs that it would bite prior to the attack.

There are exceptions when an owner is not liable, which include the dog being provoked by the injured person, but for the most part the dog owner will be held liable under Arizona law. In an effort to protect the public, Arizona law holds a dog owner responsible for his/her dog biting a person, but only if a lawsuit is filed or settlement is achieved in the first year following the attack.

If a lawsuit is not filed against the dog owner in the first year, the second - more typical - law of negligence applies. In other words, if a lawsuit is filed in the second year following the attack, but before the two year deadline, the victim must prove that the owner of the dog knew - or should have known - that the dog may bite someone. The law that automatically holds the dog owner responsible for the dog bite is no longer applicable after the first year. Having to prove that the dog owner knew the dog had a propensity to bite someone can be very difficult. In short, it is important to know that the date in which a case is filed for a dog bite claim can be the difference between a successful recovery and no recovery, at all.

CONSTRUCTION INCIDENTS

We all know working in the construction field comes with a risk of injury; however, sometimes injuries that occur are entirely preventable. Most construction accidents occur on the job site, which means the injured victim is almost always protected by workers' compensation laws. Workers' compensation laws can provide some level of recovery to the injured victim. In general, workers' compensation laws do not make the person "whole" again.

An area of construction injuries that is often overlooked is the third party liability on a construction site. Most construction sites include the work of many different subcontractors. The fact that subcontractors are working at a construction site does not relieve them of their obligation to act carefully. The obligation to always keep the site reasonably safe under the circumstances is sometimes ignored. Due to the nature of construction work and job sites, many people needlessly are seriously injured as a result.

If a worker is injured by the negligent actions of an employee who works for a different subcontractor, the injured worker will often have two remedies under the law. First, the worker has the ability to seek workers' compensation, which is a good idea to pursue in almost all of these cases.

Second, the worker can pursue a personal injury claim against the worker/company that caused the injury. This will help pay for the many items not covered by workers' compensation. This allows the injured worker to be "made whole" with all wages lost getting reimbursed in addition to other compensation available under worker's compensation laws.

PRODUCT LIABILITY

Product liability cases often receive a lot of media attention, though statistically very few product liability cases are filed each year compared to other injury cases. These cases are often based upon allegations that a product was negligently designed or manufactured. The claim is based upon an allegation that someone was injured as a result of the defective product. For instance, probably the best known product liability cases are related to the Ford Pinto, where Ford was sued for sending a car into the market where Ford allegedly knew of the dangerous propensities of that car to explode if involved in a collision.

Pursuing a product liability case is expensive and time consuming. Unlike most lawsuits that revolve around a single action, product liability cases put a lot more on the line for a defendant. If a product is found to be defective that often means there are thousands - or millions - of that same product already out in the marketplace. As a result, the defendant will often take every precaution, sparing no expense, to try to defend the product's safety. This no-holds-barred defense is not limited to the defense of safe products. This type of effort to defend a product can be seen even where the product is ultimately determined to have been an unreasonably dangerous product.

In these cases, understanding the laws of a product liability action can determine the outcome of a claim. For instance, product liability cases are not evaluated by traditional negligence principles that apply in automobile accident claims. Instead, product liability cases are evaluated on a "strict product liability" basis. In most negligence cases, the focus of the law is on the choices and actions of the defendant. However, to protect the public from dangerous products, the focus shifts in a product liability case. In a strict liability action, the focus is on the product itself, not on the manufacturer's conduct. This may seem like a small issue, but this principal can change the entire outcome of a case. Understanding the experts to hire and issues that must be addressed in these cases, therefore, starts with making sure all evidence collected and presented are focused on the appropriate issues and laws.

SLIP AND FALL/TRIP AND FALL INCIDENTS: PROPERTY OWNER LIABILITY? NOT AS OFTEN AS SOME BELIEVE

If there is any area where the belief as to what the law is by the average person differs most from what the law actually is, it is in the area of "premise liability." Premise liability is basically the responsibility a property owner has to someone who is on their property. This usually – but not always – is a case where someone is hurt because the condition of the property contributes to a "slip and fall" or "trip and fall" injury.

It seems to be the belief of most people that if they are injured on someone else's property, the property owner is legally responsible. This belief is not the law in Arizona. In Arizona, an injured person is required to show that the owner or possessor of the property is negligent, and that the negligence caused the injury.

The most common "premise liability" call we receive from an injury victim comes from the person who was walking down the grocery store aisle and slipped and fell on something that was spilled on the ground. These people have sometimes suffered significant injuries. We suspect most people who slip and fall are not seriously injured. Thus, we probably do not hear from the vast majority of people who simply pick themselves up off the ground and move on. We would guess the biggest injury they often suffer is a small bit of embarrassment.

Most people believe that if there is spilled milk, spilled juice, or something else leaking on the ground in a supermarket that the supermarket is responsible for their injury. Often times, a supermarket floor will have a clear liquid on it that is not detected by the shopper. In these cases, most people are convinced that the legal responsibility lies with the supermarket.

This often is not an accurate assumption. In Arizona, as in many states, a property owner is only liable for their own negligence. If another customer spilled water 30 seconds before the injury victim turned the corner into that aisle and fell, it is going to be difficult for anyone to believe that the supermarket should have discovered the spilled water, marked it off and cleaned it up, all in 30 seconds. In other words, under Arizona law it has to be proven that either someone from the supermarket spilled the substance or that the supermarket knew or should have known that the spilled liquid was on the aisle and had time to clean it up.

Herein lies the difficulty. Usually, nobody knows who spilled the clear juice, the milk, the eggs, or whatever else was on the ground that caused the fall. It may well have been another customer. In most cases, it is impossible to prove who spilled and how long the spill had been on the ground. Because it is unknown whether it was an employee or a customer who spilled the substance, and because it is often difficult to prove whether the injury-causing condition (the water, for instance) had been there for a period of seconds or minutes, there is very often no case. Since there usually is no evidence of how long the spill was there, we sometimes try to look to other avenues, such as reviewing the store's cleaning inspection logs to show whether or not there was a pattern of regular inspections or when the last time was that the aisle was cleaned.

Could the law be written differently so that the consumer who was injured was better protected? It could, but this is a policy decision our legislature made as to whether or not we want to spread those losses among everyone who shops at various stores or whether or not the injured person should bear the brunt of the financial losses – medical bills, lost wages, and so forth – that come from those injuries.

Suffice to say the belief that premise liability cases are simple cases for the injury victim is not usually the case. They are often difficult to prove, and almost always require a detailed investigation in order for there to be any chance at a viable claim.

Premise liability cases also have many complexities because Arizona analyzes cases based upon the legal status of the injury victim. For instance, an injured customer at a store is considered an "invitee" under the law, and thus there is a different set of requirements to have a claim than someone who is hurt at an apartment complex, who in many cases is considered a "licensee." Thus, while the specific requirements are very much dependant on these categories, generally speaking a premise liability case exists where it can be proved:

1) Somebody had an incident on property (slip and fall, trip and fall, or some other way) as a result of the condition of the property;

2) That the property was in an unreasonably dangerous condition; and

3) That the owner or possessor of the property knew, or should have known, of the unreasonably dangerous condition.

As you now know, from the earlier discussion in this book, there are four legal elements that almost all personal injury cases must have to be pursued under the law. In addition to those requirements, for premise liability cases the above three elements are all required to be proven whenever a landowner is a potential defendant in a premise liability case. These three elements simply combine to meet the first requirement of any personal injury case of proving that another party was negligent.

Since each of the above three requirements must be proven to prevail in a premise liability claim, we have discussed them separately below.

PREMISE LIABILITY REQUIREMENT #1: PROVING SOMEBODY HAD AN INCIDENT ON PROPERTY AS A RESULT OF THE CONDITION OF THE PROPERTY

Incidents on property often go undocumented, which is not surprising considering the nature of the event. In a traffic collision, cars are damaged and the need to call the police – or at least a tow truck – is often understood by everybody involved. On the other hand, people fall on a regular basis. Many times, a fall will cause some transient pain, but ultimately get better, such as a sprained ankle or bruised knee. Thus, when somebody is injured on property, the idea of calling an ambulance, calling security, or in some way documenting the event before leaving the scene is often not even considered.

Unfortunately, we have had many people call us after they have fallen and been hurt, but they simply left the scene of the event believing the injury would be minor. In leaving, they put their case in a position where there is no documentation of the cause of the fall. Such lack of documentation would include not having photographs, witness' personal information, witness statements, or written reports of the injury. Further, leaving the scene prevents the owner/possessor of the land to see what was present at the scene of the incident.

By the time these well-meaning people later realize the injury was more severe than they had thought or expected, the chance to even prove where they were injured – let alone trying to discover if there was any negligence on the part of the property owner – has already long passed.

Obviously, we have had the chance to successfully investigate these matters after-the-fact. Sometimes, we are able to reconstruct the incident, and still allow for a fair recovery to our client. Unfortunately, the longer the time period from the incident until the investigation, the greater the likelihood that key evidence will be lost and the claim will never be able to be proven.

PREMISE LIABILITY REQUIREMENT #2: PROVING THAT THE PROPERTY WAS IN AN UNREASONABLY DANGEROUS CONDITION

Whether the injury causing condition was "unreasonably dangerous" is not an easy question to answer, which is why it is left to the jury in most cases. In other words, what one person may consider unreasonably dangerous, another person may not even consider a hazard. Is a wet floor an unreasonably dangerous condition if there are no signs around to warn people? Probably. What about a backyard pool with no fence? A crack in the sidewalk that is 4 inches high? What about a crack that is two inches high?

You may feel like it would take a photograph – at least – to determine if you felt a condition was unreasonably dangerous. That may be true, but the reality is that a dangerous condition is, like art, in the mind of the beholder. This creates uncertainty for everybody involved, and any lawyer that has handled these for a period of years has grown to understand the complexity of proving an "unreasonably dangerous condition."

Thus, defining with certainty what constitutes an unreasonably dangerous condition may be impossible. Some examples, therefore, may include conditions such as:

1) Clear liquid spilled on the floor

2) Poor lighting in a dark area

3) Uneven concrete surfaces

4) Water leaking from wall or ceiling onto a tile floor

5) A rotted bleacher breaking while someone is sitting on it

6) An item falling off the shelf at a store, onto the person walking below

7) A mopped floor without any warning signs

8) A poorly designed or maintained piece of property

9) An improperly wired property that causes electrocution or electric shock

PREMISE LIABILITY REQUIREMENT #3: PROVING THAT THE OWNER/POSSESSOR OF PROPERTY KNEW OR SHOULD HAVE KNOWN OF THE CONDITION

Like many things in the law, demonstrating whether an owner or occupier of property knew or should have known about a condition can often be a matter of what people end up on the jury on that particular day.

The easier part of this equation is where the owner did, in fact, know about the existence of the condition. Most commonly, this is learned by obtaining prior written complaints relating to the condition. Sometimes, that can be shown by witnesses nearby who had complained, verbally or in writing, before the event. In many states, including Arizona, the owner is deemed to have "known" of the condition if he created it. Thus, if an owner or an employee mopped the floor, as a matter of law, he/she "knew" of the condition. Sometimes, an honest owner will admit he or she was aware of the condition.

Far more difficult is determining if an owner "should have known" about a dangerous condition. How soon after a customer spills water on the ground "should" the market find the condition? Ten hours? 1 hour? Ten minutes? The answer to this question not only varies greatly from person to person, but usually has many sub-elements that need to be considered: How big is the store? Where was the spill? How "open and obvious" was the condition? How often did the employees inspect the area? Were they required to keep "sweep logs" or in some other way document that they were taking reasonable precautions to protect their customers?

Thus, while there are many questions that the law answers decisively, some of the elements that are required to be proven under the law in premise liability cases can be uncertain, even if all the parties agree on the underlying facts.

PROPERTY DAMAGE CLAIMS ONLY

As mentioned earlier, a property damage claim, standing alone, is not a "personal injury" claim. However, because so many injury victims have a property damage claim due to the related auto accident, it is worth understanding the issues that are unique to property damage claims. To discuss property damage/car damage claims, let us use the example of Mr. John Public who is driving his car on his way to work. Somebody runs a red light and runs into his car. The damage to his car is so extensive it would cost more to repair the car than it would to simply replace the car. Let's also assume that in this scenario the driver of the other car admits that she just made a mistake. She did not intend to run the red light but she wasn't paying attention.

So, since the at-fault party with sufficient insurance coverage admits she made a mistake, can Mr. Public assume that he is going to have a situation where he does not lose money on his car as a result of the negligent actions of somebody else? Not even close.

The way the law works is that the insurance company is only responsible to pay for the "market value" of the vehicle. In other words, if Mr. Public's car was worth $25,000.00 if he had sold it in the newspaper or online that same day, that's how much the insurance company owes. Does that sound fair? At first blush it may sound fair, but the truth is in many cases it can leave the innocent victim of somebody else's neglect behind the eight ball. Let's discuss some examples.

As soon as somebody buys a new car and drives it off the dealership lot, the vehicle immediately decreases in value. We all know this. It becomes a used car. So if a vehicle is purchased for $30,000.00 let's assume that it immediately has a value of only $25,000.00. But the person who bought the car bought it for $30,000.00. If Mr. John Public drives off the dealership lot and is immediately struck by the negligent person running a red light, he is only going to receive $25,000.00 in compensation. That means he's going to owe $5,000.00 on a car that he had for less than one day when everybody agrees he did nothing wrong.

Is that fair? Why is John Public not entitled to recover the amount he owes on the vehicle instead of the amount that he could sell the vehicle for. Under our scenario we can probably assume - and let's assume it could be proved - that Mr. John Public had no intention to sell this vehicle. He had just bought it. Why does he owe $5,000.00 and lose his car. But it can be worse.

Let's assume John Public had just put $10,000.00 down on this car. He had saved $10,000.00 in order to buy this new car. He drives it off the lot and now it's hit. Now he lost the $10,000.00 that he had saved up for a down payment. Or, $10,000.00 that he had of value from a trade-in vehicle. So before the negligent person ran the red light and caused him to lose his vehicle, he had been able to have money with a down payment to buy a new car. Unless Mr. Public's in good financial standing, he is going to be taking the bus for a long time.

Who benefits from this? Well, the insurance industry. This way they're not responsible for the effect it had on John's life, only the "market value" of the vehicle.

Are there other examples of this? More than we can possibly name. What about the person who just put brand new tires on their vehicle. Undoubtedly adding new tires to a vehicle adds more value to the vehicle. But when you go to resell a car with new tires it doesn't add the complete value of the money you just spent on those tires. So you can have someone who just spent $800.00 on brand new tires and the very next day they're involved in this collision.

What are they going to do with the now "used" tires that are on a vehicle of a different size and weight of whatever vehicle he may replace it with? Realistically, he is completely out of the money he saved up and spent. Why? Because the tires are part of the vehicle and only the "market value" of the vehicle has to be paid for by the insurance company. Mr. John Public is out all the cash he just spent on those new tires. He gets almost no benefit from them. He's in a terrible position.

There are so many examples of this that it's impossible to name. Some people are "upside down" on their car not because it's a new car, but because they did not have good credit. In the attempt to dig themselves out of bad credit but still have a car to get themselves to and from work each day, they had to buy a car for more than its "market value." Well, perhaps these people in many cases contributed to the situation they're in. But even if that's true, they did nothing wrong to cause the collision in our scenario. Yet the law punishes them for being in the wrong place at the wrong time. The victim is punished once again to make sure the profits of the insurance industry increase.

Keep in mind, also, that sometimes it's a close call as to whether a vehicle is a "total loss" or whether it can be repaired. Now considering the fact that in most cases the "at fault" party is clear cut (obviously not always) there are many times where the person who did nothing wrong is in a situation where their car could either be repaired or replaced. Should the owner of the vehicle have any say in this process? If the cost of repairing the vehicle is 20 percent less than the cost of a new car, shouldn't the owner of the car have the right to insist upon the vehicle being repaired? The reality is that the law gives the at fault party complete decision making power over whether to provide "market value" cost of replacing the vehicle or whether to repair it.

The icing on the cake? These issues are rarely litigated. People need their car. When they're being taken advantage of by an insurance company they're not given a realistic option to take that case to trial. If you do not have your vehicle for two years and then you win in court two years later, what good is it? These issues are rarely litigated so that they can be abused and the laws can be manipulated to the benefit of the insurance industry.

LOSS OF USE OF YOUR VEHICLE

Why do insurance companies sometimes delay in providing a rental car when they're required to do it by law? Because, they can. Because that delay will almost never be taken to trial. There are very few lawyers that are willing to spend their time, effort and energy on a case based purely on principle, and just as few clients who, in the end, are willing to do that.

Why is it that the insurance companies are allowed to make any ridiculous offer on a total loss vehicle and at that same time pull the car rental? Same reason. Because nobody's going to fight it and, if they fight it, there's not enough of a threat to the insurance company for it to matter. Unless the laws allow for the equivalent of a "bad faith" lawsuit against insurance companies that purposely abuse the system to punish the already-victimized people who are not their own insureds, some insurance companies will continue to abuse the process.

Perhaps this is a good time for us to remind everybody that this is not to suggest that insurance companies are inherently evil. But, an insurance company will act as almost anybody will act when they are free to do so without repercussion. When an insurance company can make extra profits in violation of the law because, in the end, nobody's going to force them to do otherwise, that's exactly what they're going to do. If there are no consequences to an action, you can expect that action to take place if it is in the best interests of the actor.

DIMINUTION IN VALUE

In Arizona there is something called a "diminution of value" claim allowed under the law. This is not a claim that's allowed in every state, although it certainly should be. The way a diminution of value claim works is that if somebody is driving a vehicle and it is involved in an accident, we can expect that vehicle will have a lower resale value.

Let's use Mr. John Public who is driving his brand new $30,000.00 vehicle down the street. Two weeks after buying the vehicle somebody runs a red light and causes extensive damage. But there is only $12,000.00 worth of damage to the car so, instead of having to replace the vehicle, the insurance company is allowed to simply repair it. When Mr. John Public goes to sell that vehicle, we all know the vehicle is worth less than it would have been if there had been no accident. Let's face it, what's the first question you ask when you buy a used car?

Because the vehicle had been in a collision it will simply not be worth the same on resale, no matter how well it was repaired. So, the insurance industry is theoretically required to compensate people for the lost value, "diminution of value," of their vehicle. Is this done? All the time. Is the proper and fair and reasonable amount paid for by insurance companies? Very often fair compensation goes unpaid.

Once again, a lawsuit would have to be brought in order to fight over this disagreement. So where a proper diminution of value claim may decrease the value of a vehicle by $3,000.00 or $4,000.00, there is simply no incentive for the insurance company to settle that case at fair value. If the vehicle's been decreased in value by $4,000.00 and the insurance company offers $2,000.00, is somebody going to bring a lawsuit over that $2,000.00 difference? Rarely.

To top it all off, how can somebody prove exactly how much less their vehicle is worth as a result of an accident? Guesswork is not allowed in our legal system. You have to offer up evidence. Proof. Therefore, an expert witness is usually required who can survey the market and give explanations and facts to support the fact that there is a loss of value to the vehicle. And, more importantly, to provide exactly what that loss value is. That expert witness costs money. Is it worth hiring an expert witness, even one who tries to make himself affordable, for a claim of this size? Often, it is not, but these decisions need to be made on a case by case basis.

MISTAKE #2

FAILING TO PURSUE AN INJURY CLAIM GREEDY PLAINTIFFS, EVIL INSURANCE COMPANIES...

Personal injury victims are ordinary people. For some reason, many people have difficulty accepting the simple proposition that it is acceptable for a negligent defendant to be held responsible for his actions. Instead of agreeing with the premise of personal accountability, the following sentiment seems to us to be the norm:

All personal injury plaintiffs are greedy people just out for a quick settlement. Their lawyers care only about money, and these personal injury lawyers will take any case – good or bad, just or unjust – to line their pockets with cash.

Wrong. Wrong. Wrong. The entire paragraph above is a bunch of nonsense, even though all of the sentiments have become so engrained in the consciousness of most Americans, it is hard to have a rational conversation about this topic. There are so many one-liners and empty slogans that have filled the debates concerning personal injury lawsuits. But these beliefs are wrong in the vast majority of cases.

Unfortunately for those that have become the innocent victims of another's carelessness, there continues to be a feeling throughout this country that people who file lawsuits are greedy people. In our view, from personal experience, we know that this skepticism projected onto the innocent victim is total, complete, utter nonsense.

Innocent victims are entitled to justice.

Are there plaintiffs who lie? Of, course. Are there people that fake their injuries or sue people they know to be innocent of any wrongdoing? We are sure that type of greedy behavior exists. Is that greed the norm when it comes to personal injury cases? Let's get real.

SOMETIMES BAD THINGS HAPPEN TO GOOD PEOPLE

Personal injury plaintiffs are simply your neighbor, your co-worker, your family member, or your friend. We have fought for more than 1,000 injury victims, and the day before they became a victim of someone else's negligence, they were not personal injury plaintiffs. They were just people.

Getting hurt by someone else and needing money for medical bills, lost wages, and other legally compensable losses does not turn someone into a greedy, lying, untrustworthy person. These people were the same family members, friends, and co-workers they were the moment before someone else altered their life. Honest people are no less likely to be victims than dishonest people. Greedy people are no more prone to being victims than charitable people.

People are honest most of the time. People are straightforward and fair most of the time. Yet, as soon as somebody makes a claim that they were hurt and that they are thus entitled to money for medical bills, wage loss or – heaven forbid – "pain and suffering," there is suddenly a huge veil of suspicion and doubt about their character. As if, somehow, simply demanding fairness and accountability from an at-fault person should cast the honesty of the victim in doubt.

Someone who has been injured by the negligence of another person should not feel ashamed to pursue their claim. Pursuing a claim is the only way a victim can be compensated for their loss. It is the only way someone can be made whole.

Like it or not, money damages from the at-fault person, company, or insurance company is the only thing that can be requested in our legal arena. Someone who makes a mistake should pay for that mistake, but permanent injuries cannot be undone. Nobody owns a "magic wand." Thus, money is the only thing these victims can request, and they should not be belittled and vilified as a result.

A LAWSUIT OR A SHOTGUN: WHICH IS THE BETTER CHOICE?

If someone takes advantage of you, you have every right to fight for your rights and try to get just compensation. If you are injured, you have every right to have someone there to protect your rights. It's in your best interest. Of course, some people claim that they will never file a lawsuit against anyone, under any circumstances. Don't try to convince us of this.

As lawyers fighting for the injured every day, we know that it is easy to believe that "you" would "never" hire a lawyer. Many people that believe they would not bring a personal injury lawsuit under any circumstances are people that have been fortunate enough to never suffer a terrible injury that was caused by someone else.

First off, what someone thinks they would do as the victim of another's negligence and what they actually do is often two very different things. We cannot count the number of people who sat in front of us at an initial consultation saying, almost ashamed of being in our office, that they are not "that type" of person and they would "never sue" someone if they had not been placed in their "unique" situation. Ummm, yeah. Nobody thinks they are the type to bring a personal injury lawsuit, because almost everyone is convinced that only the rare, greedy, slimy person would do such a thing. In fact, most people who are willing to stick up for themselves would bring a personal injury claim under the wrong, unfortunate set of conditions.

What those circumstances are – whiplash vs. severe injury, bad offer vs. no offer at all – certainly varies from person to person. But ultimately, if you are not going to let someone take advantage of you and provide the compensation they are required to provide under the law, there are only two options: a shotgun or a lawsuit.

The shotgun method would definitely have a certain feeling of justice to it, and it may suit the "instant gratification" crowd quite well. However, since it often leads to long jail sentences, the courts (and lawyers) are the only other option!

Those who criticize people who file suits do not seem to realize that you cannot force a defendant into a fair settlement without filing a lawsuit. There are only two ways that a dispute can get resolved when it relates to somebody who caused a serious injury to someone else. One way that type of case can be resolved is through a settlement between the parties. That usually occurs where the insurance company and the injured party agree to what amount of money will provide fair compensation to the person who was hurt. Sometimes settlements happen without a lawsuit ever being filed. Other times, a settlement occurs after a lawsuit has been filed, but before the case goes to trial.

For instance, in our practice, we are able to achieve a settlement for our client in more than 90% of our cases. Since we are more willing to take the fight all the way to trial for the deserving client, we probably take a higher percentage of personal injury cases to trial than most lawyers. In other words, the injury victim who is willing to "fight the good fight" is far more likely to achieve an agreeable settlement – at long last – than those who simply are unwilling to defend their right to fair compensation for their losses. So, why is there such a prevailing belief that the greedy party is the one who files the lawsuit?

Many times a lawsuit is filed because the defendant who caused the injury refuses to simply pay fair compensation as required under the law. Other times, a lawsuit is filed where a defendant refuses to accept any responsibility at all for their negligent conduct.

If you had a car worth $50,000.00 and it was destroyed by somebody else, and that other person admitted that they destroyed your $50,000.00 car, but only offered to pay $11,000.00 to repair it, would you accept that amount?

If you did not accept the $11,000.00 to repair your $50,000.00 car, what would you do? Well, short of getting yourself in trouble with the law by taking matters into your own hands, the answer is you would file a lawsuit. At that point, you would be a "plaintiff."

If the same scenario took place but you had $50,000.00 in medical bills and the at-fault person only offered to pay $11,000.00, you would now be a "personal injury plaintiff."

The bottom line is that the innocent victim who defends himself from being taken advantage of, who fights to be fully compensated, or who seeks the advice of an attorney is not greedy. Often times, it is just the opposite. The people willing to seek counsel and protect themselves from injustice are more often the people who end up getting fair compensation. Getting what is owed under the law is not greed. The party who refuses to pay what they owe, on the other hand, squarely falls into the "greedy" category, in our view.

At this time, we can't do anything about the perception of those who file lawsuits; however, as more and more people continue to be taken advantage of by an often times out-of-control insurance industry and a set of laws so often adverse to the average person, we hope that injury victims who file lawsuits will be looked at for what they are: people in a dispute who have a right to be heard in court, with no presumption as to which side is right or wrong until the evidence is presented. It is time to get rid of the false presumption that a "plaintiff' is less honest, less deserving, or less fair-minded than the defendant. Society will realize that plaintiffs are just fighting for themselves as time goes on and more and more honest individuals continue to fight for their rights.

PLAINTIFF'S PERSONAL INJURY LAWYER

We understand this feeling that being a plaintiff, or being associated with personal injury at all, may be felt to be a bad thing. Consider our own story.

It took Mark years to admit he was a personal injury lawyer due to his own perception about "plaintiffs" and personal injury lawyers. He would make up all sorts of ways to describe that he was a personal injury lawyer, without ever just saying directly that this is what he did.

When asked in those early years of practice what he did for a living or what type of law he practiced, Mark would say he "helped injured people" or "helped people who have been hurt by the negligence of someone else." Mark initially could not accept the fact that he was a "personal injury lawyer." Sad to admit now, but he was embarrassed. He had seen the people on TV screaming about getting more money for clients as if they were carnival show hawkers. He had seen the phone book covers with grisly bears and sharks and who knows what other kinds of "vicious animals" the lawyers would use to represent themselves. Mark simply could not admit that he was associated in any way with those lawyers.

Even then, he was proud of the fact that he was helping people who were injured. (As an aside, he is still troubled by all of these lawyer ads with animal mascots and clients screaming, "money, money, money," but that is for another book!)

It is easier to understand Mark's unwillingness to admit he was a personal injury lawyer when you consider his perception of personal injury law when he went to law school. At that point, the idea of being a personal injury lawyer was the furthest thing from his mind. Unlike Alexis, who was raised by parents that were both lawyers and spent a lot of her early years at a little desk in a law office, when Mark went to law school he did not know anything about personal injury lawyers other than what he had seen on television. Alexis was never concerned with the perception of personal injury lawyers, but Mark at first continued to struggle to simply answer the question, "What do you do for a living?"

In any case, in every law school in the country, a student has to take a class called torts. Torts is, at least in general terms, what most people refer to as personal injury. Mark had no interest in going to this class. He still remembers being frustrated at the idea that he had to go to a class as a requisite course when he was convinced he would never consider becoming a personal injury lawyer! (Let alone become co-author of the book on personal injury law!)

In any event, it is amazing how you can be confronted with facts that force you to completely change your formerly held beliefs. We remember going to Professor Bell's first class (we had not yet met each other, but we were both in that same class) where the Professor pointed out some of the changes in our society, changes for the good, that occurred because of our personal injury system. Safer products. Bad doctors being forced out of the medical industry. A whole host of lawsuits and potential lawsuits that had changed all of our lives and made our country safer for the average consumer. We were both intrigued. Although we did not decide to become personal injury lawyers and open our office after one class, it was the beginning of Mark's speedy progress towards embracing his role as a personal injury lawyer.

After fighting for more than 1,000 clients, Mark now proudly proclaims his status as a personal injury lawyer. He is proud of being a personal injury attorney and being able to accomplish the verdicts and settlements we have earned for our deserving clients.

Lawyers help achieve justice for those who have been injured and in doing that many times we make the world a safer place for all of us. We are proud of being able to help people through the most difficult time in their life and being a meaningful part of their lives. We are proud of the fact that without our help, many of our clients would have had their lives completely destroyed. We can't undo the harm that was caused, but there's often a lot of good that we are able to do. So, go ahead and ask Mark what he does for a living. He will proudly proclaim, "I am a personal injury lawyer."

MISTAKE #3

FAILING TO UNDERSTAND THE RULES OF THE GAME

FIRST DOWN AND 25 TO GO

Beware: The Rules are changing.
You need to know how to protect yourself and what dangers you are protecting yourself from.

As we write this book, the New England Patriots have appeared in 4 of the last 7 Superbowls, winning three of them. They have been able to do this because of great players, coaching, front-office management, and an organization that has learned how to build a winner. (And possibly due to a video camera on the sidelines a few times, but we will leave that debate out of this book.)

The main reason they have been able to achieve this success is not because of all of those things, alone. They have been able to achieve this level of success because the rules of the game were the same for every team in the league. If the rules do not fairly allow for competition, the game will be altered dramatically.

Currently, every team in the NFL must gain 10 yards in 4 plays in order to be given another "first down." Since the rules are the same for every team, the better team on a given day will win in most cases. What if, however, the rules were different for some teams than for others. What if the Patriots had to gain 25 yards to get a first down, but their opponent only had to gain 10 yards? Would this be fair? Would the better team usually win? Would the Patriots have been in 4 Superbowls in the last 7 years if they had to gain 25 yards for every first down, but their opponent had to gain only 10. Not very likely.

It would be ridiculous and unfair to demand one team follow one set of rules and another team follow an entirely different set of rules. Without a fair game, the more deserving team will still lose on many days.

This analogy is applicable to what has happened in personal injury cases. The insurance industry and insurance defense lobby - as a whole - has the money and power to lobby for rules being changed in states all across the country. They have the influence to affect policy. They also have the money to get behind "tort reform" efforts throughout the nation, a set of laws which has changed the very basis of personal injury litigation.

Even in Arizona, where tort reform has failed, the money put into the tort reform movement seems to have been successful in changing attitudes of the average person about personal injury claimants by the use of misleading 30-second commercials and unsupported sound bites. Can one book change all of that? We do not believe it can. So, instead, our hope is to use this book to at least educate. We want people to understand not only what they are up against, but also to have some insight into how to handle playing a game where the injured person gets the ball, but the rules have changed, and it is now "first down and 25 yards to go" for the victim, while the insurance companies are playing the game facing the standard "first and 10."

NO SMOKE, NO FIRE

Understanding the history... injury victim vs. insurance companies. They are prepared. The injured victim is not.

If the laws are so unjust in so many cases, where is the uproar? Where is the anger? Where is the demand for fairness for the injury victim. We often hear that "where there's smoke, there's fire." The current lack of public push for fair laws for the injured victim is easy to understand. On the one side we have defendants. Most defendants who will actually become financially responsible for a negligent act that causes injury will be defendants on a regular basis. Insurance companies are in the business of defending lawsuits. They exist for the protection of their insureds. Thus, the insurance companies have every incentive to invest money, time, effort, and energy into promoting laws that are favorable to their position.

Similarly, although to a much lesser extent, governmental entities know they will get sued. As a whole, they employ so many people doing so many activities, it is inevitable that their employees will, on occasion, be negligent and cause injury. Every negligent act will not lead to injury, and every injury will not lead to a lawsuit, but the fact that a large City or State will be sued is a near-certainty.

This puts government in a position to want to protect its resources (i.e. money) and to work for rules in its favor. Herein lies the kicker . . . the government creates the rules that apply to it. If the Detroit Lions were allowed to fix the rules of the game, they would go undefeated. (OK, maybe the Lions would still find some way to lose the game, but you understand the point.)

What about injury victims? They are in a completely different position. Nobody knows if they will ever be seriously injured due to the negligence of another. In fact, the vast majority of people (thank goodness) will never be seriously hurt, let alone seriously hurt due to someone else's bad decisions. So there is no reason for most people to fight hard to change laws that will probably never apply to them. We all have enough issues that directly affect our lives, so it is difficult to get riled up over something that, as far as we know, will never affect us or somebody close to us. By the time people do become victims, it is too late to change the law.

Is anybody fighting against the insurance industry, government, and big business? Sure, the trial lawyers. But, in spite of the belief of many, most trial lawyers that help the injured are part of very small firms. Most do not have the money or time to fight for the cause . . . they are too busy fighting for their current clients in a system that is set against achieving a fair outcome. "First and 25" will keep the average personal injury lawyer pretty busy.

Even the few State and National groups that are trying to fight for injury victims are grossly outmanned. The smallest insurance company has billions of dollars in assets, far more than the groups that are fighting for injury victims. So, how can the rules be changed? How can the playing field become level? That is not an easy answer. From our end, we hope this book provides enough information to at least be a beginning point for some. Finally, it's worth noting that every jurisdiction has different laws.

The problems that our clients face are not exactly the same as clients in other states. However, the general trend against the injured is a nationwide phenomena. The decreasing jury verdicts based upon the idea that all of personal injury plaintiffs (and their lawyers) are suspicious, or greedy, or worse, is happening throughout the country.

Also worth noting is the fact that even the laws of Arizona are constantly changing. One chapter of this book was deleted between the time of the first draft and the time of the second draft, due to a change in the law. Maybe we will see more changes in the future that help the victims get back to the days of a fair fight.

THE DEATH OF AN INJURY VICTIM BENEFITS THE ADVERSE INSURANCE COMPANY

Our legal system has been created to allow people who are seriously injured to recover fair compensation for those injuries. So why is it that the same system is set up to allow the death of that person to potentially be a windfall to the insurance company they were going against?

Imagine somebody who is badly burned over their body due to a dangerous product being sold to them by a defendant. Imagine the terrible physical anguish and pain of going through skin graft after skin graft because somebody else did not care enough to spend the extra money to ensure it was selling a safe product. Imagine that person spending three years in the legal system fighting for their rights.

Now, understand the biggest part of that person's claim is probably the right to be compensated for the severe physical pain that they have endured. We have grown to almost hate the term "pain and suffering." We think it's become synonymous with the perceived abuse of our litigation system. But we don't think anyone could question in this actual scenario that the pain endured by somebody with serious burn injuries is horrendous.

We expect that almost everybody would agree that if a product was in fact unnecessarily dangerous and marketed with the full knowledge that it was dangerous, that the company should be required to pay not just for the medical bills, but to compensate the person who has suffered repeated severe constant pain.

But if four weeks before trial that badly injured person dies, the claim for damages for suffering all of that pain is extinguished and written off under the law. So a loving mother who spent three years fighting a good fight but who dies a month before trial will not be able to pass on that compensation to her children. "Pain and suffering" damages die along with the plaintiff. However there are many other claims that as personal injury attorneys we are able to present to the jury or defendant's insurance company.

GOING TO EXTREMES: LAWS THAT FAVOR FOREIGN CORPORATIONS OVER AMERICAN CITIZENS

How far do some laws go to benefit potential defendants over the injured. In our view, sometimes laws are simply offensive to the average person . . . if the average person knew they existed. One example of this occurred recently in a decision by the Arizona State Supreme Court. They ruled, in spite of a system protecting people in product liability cases for decades and which has been adopted in almost every state in this country, that in order to sue for a dangerous product, the consumer who was injured was required to sue everybody who was involved in that product for their own "individual" fault.

We are not going to pretend that we can properly explain the depth of the legal issue in this book. In truth, it could probably take a book unto itself to properly discuss how the State Supreme Court came to its conclusion and why it is so objectionable. However, we want to show an example of just how bad this law is and why we always need lawyers willing to fight to overcome these types of decisions.

Imagine a situation where the parents of a 2 year old go to the store and buy a toy at a big-box retailer for their child to play with. The child plays with the toy and, unbeknownst to them and probably unbeknownst to the retailer, the toy has lead paint that was put on the toy in China. The child swallows the lead paint and suffers a permanent brain injury. So, now we have a 2-year-old child with permanent brain damage because of lead paint improperly put on in some Chinese factory. Can anything undo this horrendous harm? Of course not. But should somebody have to pay for that child's care and at least try to make that person's life as comfortable as possible as a result of this horrendous act. Absolutely!

It has been the law in this country for a long time that the person who sells that dangerous product is required to pay for the damages caused. This is because the retailer has the ability to make decisions that will protect it financially. The retailer can buy insurance for any lawsuits that exist. The retailer can force every supplier of products it buys from to have insurance.

In contrast, the poor couple who buys the toy has no way to protect themselves. They are at the mercy of a company who sold them the product. They rely on the store they purchased the product from to sell a safe product. When someone shows up at a retailer down the street, they don't know which factory in Communist China created the product. They don't know who designed the product. They have no access to that person or company and nor do they care. They trust the retailer from whom they buy their goods and, in this example, their toys in the United States.

Now imagine a situation where when it is time to file the lawsuit, that couple can only receive compensation from the factory in Communist China that wrongfully put the lead paint on the toy. What are they going to do? Why would whatever factory that exists in China even answer their legal complaint? Who cares if they get a huge judgment against this company in Communist China? Is the company ever going to pay them? Probably, not.

By forcing retailers to be responsible for the goods they sell, the consumers in our country and, in this case, in the State of Arizona are protected. By forcing consumers to sue anyone who is a part of the process, they basically strip the rights away from the citizens of this state and of our country they are required to protect. We hope the Supreme Court reviews and changes their current decision on the law of product liability cases.

IGNORANCE OF THE LAW IS NO EXCUSE – SECRETS OF THE COURTROOM

In jury trials that occur daily throughout our great nation, there are rules of evidence employed to prevent jurors from knowing all of the facts in the case. We personally disagree with many of these rules. We even disagree with the few evidentiary rules that keep out facts which may benefit the defendant. We think jurors should be provided access to almost all of the available facts that underlie a case. Then, the jurors should be provided guidance as to what the legal issues are and how some of those facts they learned should be considered for certain purposes, and then we can trust our juries to apply all of the facts to the law. In other words, trust the jury to do the right thing.

During trial, as trial lawyers we are often prevented from telling the jurors some facts that we believe are important to the case. Trial lawyers on both sides are prevented from even telling the jurors that there are facts being hidden from them, leaving jurors to believe they have been provided all of the facts in the case. While we are unable to educate the jurors in a courtroom, we are not precluded from educating those same people outside of the courtroom: right here and now. This is an opportunity to learn some of the categories of "secrets" kept from the jury in many personal injury cases.

We have heard it said many times that our system of justice is the greatest in the world. We will accept that statement at face value, although we have never studied the differing justice systems of the world. However, having the greatest system of justice does not make it even-handed or fair, and it certainly does not mean it is perfect.

It is time to strip away at least some of these "hidden rules" and legalities that force injured people to do more than just "prove their case." It is time to expose the places where the justice system fails to provide justice to injury victims. Let's see why it is first-and-25 for the injured, and see if we can learn enough, educate others, and resolve to make sure that the fairness afforded to defendants is equally afforded to the people that have been harmed.

EVER BEEN TO A JURY TRIAL?

Many injury victims have never set foot inside a courtroom until their own case is going to trial. The same is true for prospective jurors. It is not just our clients that have not been educated in the way a trial works until after they were hurt. Most jurors have never been a part of the legal system. The closest thing they know to the legal system is watching *Law and Order.* Many people seem to think that the legal shows on television accurately portray the way a trial works. Some of these shows about lawyers manage to take 2-3 cases from start to finish, including a trial, in each episode. That is a far cry from the way our civil justice system actually works.

This ignorance of the way the legal system works is understandable, as we all have very busy lives and a lot to do. It is also easily remedied. Our courts are a public forum. Almost every single document filed related to a personal injury case of any kind is a public record. More and more, these records can be accessed by simply spending a few minutes on the internet. At most, it takes a trip to the local courthouse to see these public documents. Also, jury trials are open to the public. Anyone can go down to the courts and watch a jury trial at any time. Seeing a trial can be an eye-opening experience, because as a citizen just watching a trial, the average citizen can see not only what the jury sees, but also observe the arguments made by the lawyers as to what facts should be kept hidden from the jury.

Of course, there is nothing wrong under the current rules of evidence with the lawyers making these arguments to preclude evidence, we have made them many times. There are rules to this game, in this case the rules of evidence, and the job of the lawyers and judge is to play within those rules. It just so happens, we would like to see the rules changed. The ability to actually watch any trial is either a well kept secret, or people know they can go but have no interest in watching actual trials as they occur. As attorneys who have tried many cases and witnessed many as well, you may be surprised to learn that there is almost nobody in the courtroom watching a typical personal injury trial. The few people you might see watching a trial are interested observers, family, friends, insurance adjusters, or somebody with some sort of stake or interest in the outcome.

For instance, in our own trials, it's not unusual to look back and see both sets of our parents watching! Mark's dad has been to some portion of almost all of our trials. It's hard to imagine that going to all your son's trials is a good way to spend retirement, but it's always great to have our parents watch our trials. However, our parents do not count as unbiased observers to the trial process.

We can remember only a few trials where a member of the public spent a significant amount of time watching the trial purely out of interest. There have been some occasions where the media was present, and other lawyers have watched us in action, but almost never do we see completely "unattached observers." Our point is that, in spite of the fact that our courts do everything they should do in keeping the trial process open to the public, the truth is that very few people have any idea what is happening in personal injury cases, and few people have the time to go and find out for themselves.

Mark's experiences when he has been summoned to be a potential juror have been very interesting. He was summoned twice for jury duty. Not surprisingly, he never made it onto the actual jury. Alexis has never been selected for a jury either. Most lawyers are afraid that allowing another lawyer to be placed on the jury will put too much power in the hands of that one person. In other words, there is a fear amongst many trial lawyers that the rest of the jurors will simply follow the lead of the lawyer who is on the jury, effectively changing the process from a trial heard by many people to a trial decided by just that one lawyer.

What Mark saw in his last trip to jury duty was a reinforcement of how so few people (potential jurors) had any idea of what was actually going on in the courtroom. In that particular instance, as is typical in most cases, the entire group of prospective jurors was called into the courtroom and asked many questions to see whether or not they would qualify to be a juror in that case. This process, called "voir dire," took about an hour and a half.

When the questioning was done, it was time for the prospective jurors to be sent out into the hall so that the judge and lawyers could decide who would be a part of the jury. Once out in the hall, Mark heard multiple people asking what was going on. He remembers one person saying she had no idea what she had just been through, or any idea what was going to come next.

We do not fault any of these people for not understanding. We really don't. We do not claim to understand the inner workings of almost anybody else's job nearly to the degree we understand the law. The problem with this basic lack of understanding is that the Courts are such a key part of our democracy. If people do not understand courts and the importance of juries, they are less likely to fight to protect this vital institution. The right to a jury trial is a central element to our democracy.

JURORS MUST PUT A "PRICE" ON SOMETHING THAT HAS INFINITE VALUE

We have had potential jurors, people called to jury duty and asked questions to see if they could be fair and impartial, stricken (sent home and not allowed to be a part of the jury) because they could not put a dollar value on an injury. At some point before almost anyone becomes a juror in a personal injury case, they are asked if they will follow the instructions and award money damages. They must award an amount based on the evidence.

A few people refuse to award money damages for anything: medical bills, lost wages, damaged property; these types of people are few and far between. On the other hand, we have had many people dismissed from jury duty because they told the judge that, even if instructed by law that they must put a dollar value on pain, suffering, distress, and loss of enjoyment of life, they refused to do so. Of course, some of these people were probably just looking for a way out of jury service!

Most of these people who said they would not award money to someone who was injured felt uncomfortable trying to put a dollar figure on those types of claims. And, you know what? We get it.

Money can pay off unpaid medical bills. A jury can require a defendant to pay money for the time lost from work, for out of pocket expenses. But money for pain? Suffering? Lost ability to enjoy life? Money will not fix those problems. No matter how much money is awarded to someone who was paralyzed due to another's neglect, the money will not allow them to walk. Regardless of the jury verdict, the person who lives with debilitating, severe headaches will continue to suffer. The family living in despair because someone's careless actions killed their family member will not get their loved one back.

So, to start with, when we are dealing with an award of money when actual dollars were not lost, and money cannot fix the problem that was created by someone else's actions, it is difficult for everyone involved. Money is the only option jurors have, however, and it is what is provided for under the legal system for personal injury victims because the jury cannot undo the harm. We will point out, however, that the idea of providing money damages due to negligence is not an American invention. Surprised?

The fact that money is awarded to compensate for these losses also partially explains why no personal injury case has a precise, certain value. The value of the case – the amount a jury will award to the injured – is always an unknown and always subject to a relatively wide range of results.

If some rational people cannot award anything even if instructed to under the law, how could the rest of us agree as to the exact, fair amount of the claim. As lawyers, we do this by predicting what we think a jury will do based on other verdicts that have been given in similar cases.

SUING THE OTHER PARTY'S INSURANCE COMPANY? NOT EXACTLY.

This is an area that varies greatly from state to state. However, in Arizona when somebody's been severely injured by a negligent driver, they are required to name only the negligent driver in the lawsuit. The fact that insurance exists is never brought to the attention of the jury. Instead, at trial you have a case of John Smith v. Jane Doe. In other words, all the jury sees is some average citizen being sued for potentially hundreds of thousands of dollars in medical bills and wage loss, perhaps millions of dollars in overall claim value. Jurors are left wondering how "Jane Doe" is ever going to be able to pay for these injuries. That is because jurors are not allowed to be told that Jane Doe has insurance. They are not allowed to know that there is insurance that will cover the verdict.

We understand the rationale behind this policy, but we simply disagree with it. We understand this fear that somehow people will award more money if they believe that there's insurance. We just don't buy it. Most people are more afraid of their insurance rates going up for awarding too much money. We think most people are sick of what they perceive to be unfair awards that benefit plaintiffs and are very much inclined to make sure they do not give too much money to a personal injury plaintiff.

It is completely unfair that somebody may receive less than the full value of their case because the jurors are afraid that the defendant will not be able to afford to pay the fair amount of compensation that should be owed. Jurors ought to know that there is an insurance company that will pay only what the jury finds to be the fair amount of compensation. The reality is that in most personal injury trials, the insurance company is the "real party in interest." In other words, it is the insurance company that is paying for the lawyer. It is the insurance company that will pay any judgment. The lawsuit should properly name the insurance company, unless money is actually being sought from the pocket of the at-fault driver.

EXPERT WITNESS VS. TREATING DOCTOR

Personal injury trials often revolve around the medical treatment received, the diagnosis of the injuries, whether those ailments were caused by the defendant, and what the long-term prognosis is for the victim. As such, the injured person will often call his treating doctors into court to testify. In response, the defendant – usually funded by the insurance company behind the case – hires a doctor of their choosing to examine the plaintiff and give opinions. Thus, jurors often times are hearing evidence from a paid expert versus a client's treating doctor. For this reason, plaintiff's lawyers often are forced to hire expert doctors as well.

Treating doctors generally aren't "gung-ho" over being called to testify at trial. The reality is that putting a hand-picked doctor up against a treating physician is not a fair fight in the courtroom. The doctors who testify on behalf of personal injury plaintiffs are most always the doctors who were chosen solely because they were on the plaintiff's health insurance plan. Or, where someone has no health insurance, the doctor was often chosen because they were willing to treat that person and then wait for payment until the case had concluded. They may be great doctors, caring doctors, affordable doctors, and convenient doctors.

However, these doctors were not chosen because they are comfortable testifying. So these treating doctors are often uncomfortable making any strong statements. They went to medical school to be medical doctors. Good for them. They should do exactly what they are good at and what they enjoy. We understand that being involved in litigation on behalf of patients is a necessary evil to many doctors. On the other hand, the defendants hire their own doctors. They hand-pick doctors who tend to be very conservative in their approaches and in their beliefs (not politically conservative, but conservative in that they never believe an injury was caused by an accident, or they do not believe that injuries are almost ever as severe as the person claims they are, and so forth) and the insurance company gets to pick doctors who are skilled witnesses and who enjoy testifying.

Is it a fair fight? It certainly is not. Can the insurance companies be blamed for hiring doctors who are skewed in their favor? No, because the law allows it. Could the law require a truly independent doctor to be chosen, one who is not hand-picked because he will testify in almost every case against the injured person? The law could certainly do that. But it does not. Could the law prevent insurance companies from hiring more than one doctor until they find a doctor who is willing to say what they want them to say? The law could do this, but it does not.

Instead, insurance companies can send around copies of a victim's medical records until they find a doctor who is willing to say exactly what the insurance company wants. They can hire that doctor and, in most jurisdictions, nobody is even allowed to know how many different doctors the insurance company had review a plaintiff's medical records until they found one doctor who would say that the injury was not caused by a particular incident.

After all that, what does the jury see? A paid, skilled, testifying expert doctor. One who was purchased with the resources of a multi-billion dollar insurance company that went "opinion shopping." Who does the jury hear from for the plaintiff? Usually the doctor who is "stuck" testifying because he was on the victim's insurance plan and located near the victim's home. Is there any way to avoid this? Sure. There are cases where we hire doctors who did not treat our clients to give opinions in an effort to level the playing field. However, the value of this is often minimized if our client's own "treating" doctor is not willing to say as much as the retained expert. It is, in the end, another built-in advantage afforded to the defendants.

WHERE THE LAW ALLOWS ABUSIVE CONDUCT TO GO UNDETERRED, EXPECT ABUSE TO OCCUR

Early in our practice we had a young couple who had been involved in a very standard automobile accident when the wife was driving to work and she was rear-ended. Her injuries were nothing more than whiplash.

So we had this young couple with a wife who had a fairly minor case of whiplash. And if it were just for that injury case, if there was nothing else going on, the case would have settled a month or two after we took it on. The twist in the case was that their vehicle had to be repaired. The insurance company arranged, probably after a fight, to allow our client to get a rental car. Considering the law requires them to provide a rental car during the time that the vehicle is being repaired, this is not exactly a gift provided by the insurance company. However, it took longer for the car to be repaired than anyone had expected. The biggest inconvenience in cases like this is not to the insurance company, but to the person who loses access to their own car. A rental car is fine and it's certainly far better than nothing. However, it's not as good as having your own car back after it's been repaired and returned to the place it was prior to the collision.

So the estimated time for repair was something along the lines of four weeks. When it hit the four-week mark and the car wasn't repaired the insurance company decided that they had expected the car to be repaired within four weeks, so they were no longer going to provide a rental car.

Imagine that. Because their forms somewhere tell them that the car should - on average - be repaired in a certain amount of time, if things take place that delay the repair through no fault of the victim, the insurance company claimed the right to simply pull the rental car from this couple. Well, it just so happens that after about four weeks of dealing with doctors and everything else, our young wife/client had gotten to the point where she was done treating with doctors and she was going to go away for a nice weekend with her husband. They had the hotel plans. They had everything set for the weekend.

It was Friday afternoon when we received a phone call from the insurance company demanding that the car be returned because this was the last day under their four-week time frame that they expected the car to be repaired. We explained that nobody had done anything wrong. In fact, the insurance company did not even allege that the body shop had done something wrong or that our client had done something wrong. Simply put, the insurance company said it was taking too long for their liking. Or, let's call it as it is, it was costing them a little bit more money than they had anticipated as a result of the negligent actions of their insured.

When we explained that at a minimum we would like our clients to be able to have three more days of this car rental we were told that if the car was not returned by 5:00 that afternoon (about two hours later) that they would report the car stolen and our clients would be arrested.

That case went all the way to a jury trial. Is that a complete waste of judicial time and resources? Probably. But here's the deal: A plaintiff is faced with two choices when the at-fault person's insurance company decides to take ridiculous stances at their expense. Many clients we have had before or since that couple when it comes to a rental car simply take what they're given and move on and we respect that decision. We respect the fact that there are bigger battles to fight in life and sometimes you're better off just moving on with your life. However, we will always respect this particular young couple for the fight they were willing to take on. But what's important beyond that anecdote is what it tells us about the laws and the way they favor the insurance companies. Because, in spite of the willingness to fight this nonsense, when we file a lawsuit regarding rental car coverage there is no cause of action against the insurance company. There were no laws that benefited our clients and allowed them to gain any extra damages as a result of what this insurance company did.

Although we fought the fight and took the case all the way to trial and won, the insurance company is a multi-billion dollar company, the "win" had no effect on their bottom line. Unfortunately, the laws do not punish an insurance company for randomly assigning dates that they're going to pull a rental car. Some of you who are more knowledgeable in this may be thinking that this is "bad faith" by the insurance company. For reasons that are too complex to get into here - but are best explained by the fact that it was not her own insurance company - this was not an act of bad faith by the adverse insurance company under Arizona law. Some other states would have allowed an "unfair claims practice" lawsuit to deter such bad behavior, but this option is generally not available to Arizona residents.

MISTAKE #4

NOT UNDERSTANDING "CASE VALUE"

It is impossible in a book to say what a personal injury case is "worth." There are too many specific circumstances involved in every individual case to draw generic conclusions. For instance, if someone is injured in a collision with a tractor-trailer, and the truck driver fell asleep because he was driving in excess of the federal guidelines, the victim may be entitled to damages to punish the driver and company. If the person who caused a collision was drunk, the case may be worth more for similar reasons. If the doctor who committed malpractice made the same mistake on a repeated basis, injuring people over and over again, this may increase the jury's motivation to make a statement, thus increasing the value of the case.

Anyone who states they can know the value of a case with just one conversation and no review of evidence is almost always just pulling numbers out of a hat. To really give an honest and professional assessment on a personal injury case, a lawyer needs to see the actual evidence – the vital documents – and investigate further.

WAITING FOR A COMPLETE RECOVERY WHENEVER POSSIBLE

First, it is important that personal injury plaintiffs wait to settle their claims until they have physically returned back to pre-injury condition, or until their healing has reached a final plateau. The need to wait to attempt settlement is based upon the reality that, in Arizona and many other states, there is only a one-time, lump sum settlement at the conclusion of the case. Once the case is settled, it cannot be re-opened to pay for medical bills that occur after the settlement or wages that are lost after the settlement. Even families that suffer the tragedy of a loved one killed by another's negligence just receive lump sum settlements.

It is important not to rush into a settlement, but to take time to gather all the necessary documents that will support the claim. Many people have been short-changed in their compensation due to a rush to get the case finished prematurely.

Once an injury case is at the point of negotiating a settlement, it is necessary to try to predict what would happen if the case were to go to trial. It is impossible to settle a case without at least trying to come to an educated guess – a hypothesis – of what a jury will do on a given case. What is common with similar cases and knowing what similarly situated cases have received from juries tells us the likely value of a given case. By relying upon experience and understanding of what other juries in that jurisdiction have determined in similar cases, we are able to arrive at a settlement value of a personal injury case. In our practice, it is this comparison to similar cases that determines the advice we give our clients regarding the settlement value of their case.

In personal injury cases, there simply is no "schedule" of injuries and what fair compensation is for those injuries. You may have heard that there are schedules that may dictate that a broken finger is worth a certain amount, if somebody lost their baby toe that is assigned a certain settlement value, and so forth. Those schedules exist, generally, in workers' compensation claims which have a totally different set of rules and laws from personal injury cases.

When it comes to personal injury cases, the value of the case is generally based upon what a particular jury is likely to award to the victim in that case. That varies greatly depending on time and place. Just like a house can be worth more or less depending on where it's located, the same is true for the fair value of a personal injury case. Let me give you some examples.

We have filed more cases in Maricopa County Superior Court than any other county. As a result, we have learned what Maricopa County jurors are likely to award in certain, similarly situated cases. And let's face it, jurors are just people brought together into the courtroom. But people don't think the same way, as a group, in all places throughout the country. For instance, we have come to expect outcomes of certain types of injury cases based upon past jury awards in Maricopa County. However, there are other counties, particularly some rural counties in Arizona, where the exact same injury with the exact same facts of the collision, with the exact same doctors, the exact same people, would tend to produce – on average – much lower verdicts.

Why is that? How can the exact same case with the same doctors and same witnesses be worth different amounts depending on where the injury took place? It's worth a different amount because juries in different places tend to give us different verdicts. A jury in New York City may give a very, very different verdict than a jury in Dallas.

Of course, there is no way to know what a given jury will do on any given day. There's no way to have absolute certainty because until the very moment the jury is sat and the case is started, you don't even know who the people are that are going to be deciding the case. Even if you knew what people were going to be deciding the case, you may not know how those people will react to the facts given to them. Since this group of people has never been a "group" before – in fact most of them have never met each other before – there's no way to know how they will make a decision as a group in that particular case.

Obviously, we are not suggesting that juries in Phoenix always do the same thing and that we can predict with certainty the outcome of a given case. If we knew the outcome of a given case, every case would settle because we would know what the jury was going to do with it. Instead, it's a reality that over time in different jurisdictions you tend to get some idea as to what the jury – on average - will do in that county compared to other counties.

So you may have the exact same case in Phoenix, Arizona as you do in Yuma, Arizona but the expected award to the injured person is very different based purely upon location. Now, it works both ways. The juries in Pima County, where Tucson is located, tend to give somewhat larger verdicts than their Phoenix counterparts. Therefore, our clients in Phoenix would have expected to receive more compensation from those juries, on average, had the negligent act occurred in Tucson instead of Phoenix. This is difficult for a lot of people to accept. Everybody wants certainty. It doesn't seem fair to most people that the pain they've gone through, the suffering, the medical bills they've incurred, the wage loss that they've had, could be valued differently depending on where the injury took place. We understand that frustration.

If you think it may be troubling in Arizona, where hundreds of miles may completely change the value of the case, consider what it must be like in the Detroit metropolitan area. Here is a story from Mark: I grew up in Detroit. When I was in law school I worked for a lawyer, Ada Montgomery, during the summer between my first and second year of law school. That's when I was really taught the importance of the county where the case was to be tried.

The Detroit metropolitan area is made up of three different counties. Two of those counties, Oakland and Wayne, are separated by a street called 8 Mile Road. The value of an injury case in Detroit can vary based on a few feet. Feet! Back when I was working for Ada, a person who was in an automobile collision in Wayne County could expect a jury far more willing to award considerable compensation for their case than if that same collision happened a few feet north of 8 mile road, in Oakland County. Imagine knowing that you would be compensated more or less, to a noticeable and significant degree – because you happen to be involved in an accident on the south side of 8 Mile Road instead of north of 8 Mile.

So, what does all this tell us? First, we know our judicial system is unpredictable. The people who blast our system use that lack of predictability to suggest that there's something wrong with our system. It's just not the case. In fact, if you talk to most judges and lawyers around the country who watch these cases go to trial on a regular basis, you would find a majority who believe that the most unpredictable verdicts are often those that go against the plaintiff as opposed to in favor of the plaintiff.

For instance, we have all heard – repeatedly – of the "McDonald's hot coffee case." Although that case was misreported and the facts were not known to most of the public, the belief in the general public is that some woman driving through a McDonald's drive-thru spilled coffee on her lap and was given millions by a jury. That is not what happened. But we can ignore that portion of the debate for the moment. What's more important is to understand that even if that was true, even if it was simply a woman who spilled some coffee on her lap and got millions of dollars – as ridiculous and nonsensical as that verdict would be – it would still be just one incident of a jury doing something unusual or strange.

What about the mother whose child dies in her arms following what almost everybody believed to be obvious and inexcusable medical neglect, only to have the jury award nothing for the loss of her son? What of the fact that these types of injustices happen every single day throughout our country. Let's face reality, it's hard to make a headline interesting when a jury awards nothing. It takes too much time to understand each individual case to realize whether an injustice was done.

MISTAKE #5

NOT DOCUMENTING EVERYTHING POSSIBLE IF IT ISN'T WRITTEN, IT DIDN'T HAPPEN

The excuse insurance companies most commonly use for failing to offer a reasonable settlement is that the injured person cannot produce any written evidence or other documented proof of their injury claim and/or other claimed losses. The insurance companies will argue lack of written evidence both prior to any lawsuit being filed and all the way through the time of closing argument in front of a jury. Their argument is that if something happened, the injured person would have written evidence to that effect. Thus, cases are not proven and won by the facts. Maybe that sounds strange, but it is the reality of our legal arena. How are claims proven and won?

They are proven and won by "the evidence" that can be shown. The truth of what happened is not enough. Of course, it is important that all injury victims tell the truth. In our office, if you are not telling the truth, or if we suspected you were not telling the truth, our office would not represent you. We doubt that is just our rule. Even before we had the ability to be as selective in the clients and cases we accepted, we would never represent anybody who we thought was lying. The fact is, there is no need for lawyers to even consider representing phonies. A very small percentage of people who claim to be injured are lying about what they have suffered.

And yet, this is the common type of abuse that happens to the injury victim. We use the example of an automobile collision now and often throughout the book. That is not because automobile collisions are the only way that negligent people cause harm to others. We know that there are many different ways that people are injured and have no recourse other than through our legal system. However, the automobile collision is something that we all can understand and relate to, and it is the simplest form of an injury case. As this book shows, that does not make it simple. So let's use some examples of this bias against the victims following a serious injury and why it is necessary that everything be in writing. Almost all people who are involved in personal injury cases had absolutely no forewarning of what they were about to suffer. In other words, it is not a situation that the injured person could have planned for.

The injury victim is just a regular person living his/her life. A woman on her way to work, a man driving his family around town, a family on their way to the grocery store, or to a baseball game. In fact, for any infinite number of places and destinations, an auto accident can happen along the way.

For example, let us take the average person, Mr. John Q. Public, driving on his way to work. He goes through an intersection and is t-boned at 50 miles an hour by a car he never saw coming. He is "out of it" for some unknown period of time. When he "comes to" from his haze, people start showing up at the scene like firemen, paramedics, and police. In some cases, witnesses even stay around to help out. Considering the fact that John Public was just on his way to work and now has his head ringing, what do you think he ought to do?

Well, Mr. John Public just found himself in a no-win situation in terms of handling a potential personal injury case. The biggest "mistake" that John can make from the standpoint of a case – if he ever is forced to bring one – will arise from his failure to document everything that has happened, starting immediately following the incident. Head ringing, paramedics helping, police interviewing and witnesses assisting while in shock is a tough time to start documenting what is going on. In the more serious injuries, it is downright impossible. Nonetheless, everything that is not documented is lost. Whenever possible, document everything! For instance, we give our clients a binder to keep everything in so the documentation is kept in one place. We encourage all injury victims to do the same. Document all that you can as soon as that is possible. It is rare that documentation hurts the injured party. It is the lack of proof that can be fatal to a personal injury victim's claim.

We recognize that it is not possible to have everything in writing. Still, whenever possible, each of the following items are critical and should be documented as soon as possible:

1. Photographs of the injury scene (showing both cars stopping position, skid marks, etc.). Take as many as possible, from as many angles as possible

2. Photos of the vehicles involved. Again, the mistake people make once they take photographs is usually taking too few. Take as many photos as you think may be needed, then take some more.

3. Debris from the scene of the incident (broken glass from the car, damaged items in the car, etc)

4. Photos of the injuries. Every bruise, scratch and cut is worthwhile to document. In some cases, there are issues relating to the biomechanics of the incident, and sometimes a certain bruise or mark on the body can prove the direction a vehicle travelled, which can help prove who was at fault. It may sound strange, but there are experts in determining what happened to the body during an incident that can use this type of information. Also, take these photos throughout the healing process, not just at the outset. Some injuries will not appear for days or longer, while others can last for weeks. Time-stamped photographs can be vital proof at a later date.

5. Photos of any items you may need because of your injury, including bed pan, cane, custom shoes, etc.

6. A brief journal kept about your injuries. This need not be a diary, but it might help capture some of those frustrating issues that others may not have considered

7. Prescriptions/scripts provided to you from doctors (including to remain off of work, to go to another doctor, etc.)

8. All receipts for costs incurred (including prescriptions, co-pays, funeral costs, etc)

9. Any disability paperwork or workers compensation paperwork

10. Names and address of witnesses if they do not appear on police report, as well as anything that you overheard any witnesses say at the scene.

11. Notes from employer or supervisor regarding missed time off work, job description, etc.

Why is it necessary to have the above documented? For instance, if John does not have any photographs of his vehicle or the other vehicle taken, a jury cannot understand the extent of damage to the vehicle. We had one case where the client was claiming he had brain damage. The defendants admitted our client needed two brain surgeries, but denied the brain injury was caused in the crash from which the case arose. Fortunately for our client, a photograph which we were able to obtain taken by the police showed the adverse party's vehicle resting on the roof of our client's car, right where his head had been before he was air-evacuated from the scene.

Not having relevant photographs can decrease the ability to obtain fair compensation from an adverse insurance company looking for any excuse, any lack of documentation to decrease the settlement offer. As the old saying goes, "a picture is worth 1,000 words." If the insurance company refuses to settle, "John Q. Public" could find himself on a witness stand being cross-examined as to what actually happened in this incident, and what he did or did not see. He will be grilled repeatedly on what he claims he saw because there is no documented "evidence." He will sometimes even be attacked for failing to take those pictures immediately.

Maybe that seems unfair. Maybe you feel like we should not demand so much of Mr. John Q. Public after all that he has been through, he should not have to worry about anything other than recovery. We agree that would be fair and reasonable. Unfortunately, the facts must be documented to be used as evidence. We would like to tell you that people are understanding of not documenting things in a personal injury claim. We would love to claim that the average jury is forgiving of this common mistake. We want to tell you that, but we cannot.

The reality is that the written word, even written by a party to the lawsuit, simply carries more weight with what people later say they remember but have not preserved beyond their own testimony.

Showing a person's swollen leg is more persuasive than telling an adjuster or a jury that the leg was swollen. Showing skid marks of the scene of the accident is more persuasive than claiming the other car began to skid prior to the crash. Having a statement from a witness is something an adjuster can read versus just telling them this is what the witness will say. Showing with a picture the inconveniences of using a wheelchair, bed pan, a cane, a shower chair, or any of the other items needed to assist with activities of daily living after an injury are things people can understand better when they see.

For most of us, the broken pieces from two cars involved in a collision have little value. Yet any experienced personal injury lawyer has seen cases draw into long, contentious disputes over something as simple as the exact location of the incident. Two parties may disagree as to whose lane of travel the crash occurred in. The parties may disagree as to what happened to the vehicles after the collision. There are any number of factors where the location of the debris from the collision could be a determining factor.

Most often, the insurance company does not tell the injured victim that these are issues that may be brought up at the time of settlement and the injured victim loses out on documenting important evidence.

For our clients, this can be a huge hurdle to overcome. If there is no evidence of what occurred that helps the defendant. The plaintiff has the burden of proof. If there is no evidence of something we claim happened that is not a "wash" for the parties, but a victory for the defendant.

Why does the insurance company defending a lawsuit get a benefit from something neither side can prove? Because the party with the burden of proof must actually "prove their case." For our purposes here, the burden of proof requires the plaintiff to "prove" what happened in a particular incident.

For example, "John Public" who just got rammed into at 50 miles an hour, whose head is spinning, who does not yet remember where he is, is not going to get out of the car, take pictures of the vehicles, and pictures of the debris on the road. What is important is that there is as much documentation as possible to later be presented to the insurance company or jury. Unfortunately, this includes attempting to foresee what documentation will be demanded by the insurance company at the time of settlement, or what will be a key piece of evidence at trial.

We know it seems somewhat uncomfortable to start documenting everything before you even know if you will be pursuing a claim, or if you do not know whether or not you will need this documentation. The documentation need not be done by the victim. It can be done by a friend, family member, or investigator brought in by a personal injury lawyer, depending upon how soon the law office is retained.

Even if someone accuses the victim of being too quick to think lawsuit and start documenting evidence, it is better to be accused of considering a lawsuit too fast than be accused of lying because you lack the documentation to prove the truth of what occurred.

MISTAKE #6

NOT HAVING OPEN AND HONEST COMMUNICATION WITH ALL DOCTORS AND FIRST RESPONDERS

EVEN ONE FAULTY ENTRY IN A POLICE REPORT CAN DERAIL A LEGITIMATE CASE

This step goes to the "causation" portion of the case we discussed earlier. As we all know, police officers go to the scene of an accident immediately. As a group, police have far better things to do (like, maybe, catch bad guys) than investigate traffic collisions.

The downside to this is that, since it is not a priority but it is often a necessary evil that officers are required to do, police reports of automobile collisions are often not as thorough, complete, or accurate as they could be. We have had many occasions where our client needed surgery but the police report inaccurately states that there were no injuries to anybody involved in the incident.

In Arizona, the State has basically made all of the different police organizations throughout the State use the same type of Arizona traffic accident report form. Regardless of which police agency shows up to investigate an accident, the report is similar. One of the things you can expect in these reports is there is an "injury code." This injury code correlates with what the police officer reports in terms of injuries (or no injuries) to the people involved. Can you think of any particular problems with the police report noting the injuries at the scene of a collision?

To start with, nobody at the scene has a crystal ball. Somebody may have adrenalin going through their system and not even realize they are hurt. Or somebody might have the type of injury that does not present itself until after the person has left the scene. Or, perhaps, a police officer who is trying to make sure that nobody at the scene is injured by a passing motorist and is trying to secure everything safely will not have the opportunity to make it his or her top priority to get the "injury code" section correct. Or maybe, just maybe, there will be miscommunication between somebody who was just knocked senseless by a 4,000 pound vehicle running into the side of his car, and will not properly relate his condition to the police officer.

Let us be clear about this. This is not a criticism of the police. The police have an important role to do. That role does include doing their best to document the "injury code." But when they show up on an accident scene, documenting things for a potential future personal injury case is just not priority number one. That is a darn good thing! Yet, here we have a major problem that occurs in Arizona and probably everywhere. The person at the scene may be asked if he feels that he is hurt. If he tells the police officer he does not think he is hurt, the officer will probably write down that there was no injury. In our traffic accident reports, this is an injury code "1." If he tells the police officer he maybe injured but he does not know, the police officer may write down a "1" or a "2" which indicates possible injury.

The fact is nobody knows with certainty what injuries were caused when they are still at the scene. Some injuries look devastating at first, but turn out to be relatively minor. On rare occasions, somebody that appears to have no injury has actually suffered a significant injury that does not present itself until later. There is no doctor on the scene. No diagnostic tests, X-ray, MRI, CAT scan, or any other tool that has been used. The person who is answering the police officer is just doing the best job he/she can under the circumstances.

The problem is the adverse insurance company and many juries put a lot of emphasis in the police report written by the police officer. Many times the victim (who minutes earlier had no reason to believe that he was going to be involved in this collision, was not mentally prepared for it, was not there taking notes, and is still getting their senses about them) is not prepared to talk to the officer. This goes back to the lesson we previously discussed: personal injury cases are decided based upon the evidence, not on all of the facts. If the code is wrong, other evidence needs to be looked at to convince the adjuster or jury that the person was more seriously injured and that the injury was caused by the accident.

MEDICAL RECORDS TWISTED BEYOND ALL RECOGNITION

How important are the medical records to a personal injury victim's case? The answer is that those written reports made in a doctor's office probably have a bigger affect on the search for justice than any other part of an injury lawsuit. Now, have you ever read your own medical records? Were they accurate?

Doctors do not create medical records for lawsuits, they create medical records to assist in medical treatment. When somebody has had a severe injury, the medical records for the care they received are voluminous. They are filled with the sometimes illegible handwritten notes from many doctors, nurses, and others who assisted in the patient's care. Mixed into the records are untold numbers of diagnostic reports of various kinds and we cannot forget the lab reports that sometimes make no sense to anybody outside of the laboratory. Nursing notes. Intake sheets. If you have never seen your own medical records, you may be surprised at what is . . . and is not . . . contained in them.

Unfortunately, unless somebody has been in the medical field – or spent time reviewing records such as working in the personal injury arena they usually do not understand just how often notations within the medical records are incorrect. The reality is that those medical records were not created in order to be picked apart, word by word, in a personal injury context. They are usually made "on the fly" or by the memory of the doctor after-the-fact. They are created to make sure the important medical issues are documented. They are often not reviewed for accuracy by the doctor or his staff, and almost never even seen by the patient to confirm the subjective complaints were accurately recorded.

A single notation from a single doctor can change the insurance company's evaluation of a case. The assumption by most people, therefore most jurors, is that the medical records will be accurate. Since somebody who claims that they have been injured is required to prove that they have been injured, the trust placed in those records becomes central to the process. If there are errors in the records, you must talk further with your doctor and request additional documentation.

THE OPPORTUNITY TO GET JUSTICE OFTEN LIES WITHIN THE RECORDS

An injured person must be honest and communicate with the doctor. Don't let the doctor guess as to how you are feeling. Let the doctor know exactly how your discomfort is affecting you every time you speak with a medical professional. Medical records are even more likely to be wrong when the patient is not communicating well with the doctor. Also, when the treatment is not consistent, medical records are even more likely to have things that are wrong, and more likely to fail to document everything adequately.

Should the records be important? Yes. Do we wish jurors knew that these records were often created "on the fly." Yes, yes, yes. Since medical records are most often not created in anticipation of litigation, the more you tell your doctor and the more you go to your doctor, the more medical documentation will be in your file documenting your injury. If there is a mistake or something is taken out of context, it is easier to prove when there are ample records showing what is really going on with your injury.

HOW ONE SENTENCE CAN FORCE A CASE TO TRIAL

We once had a mortgage broker come into our office with a severe knee injury following an automobile accident. He was actually referred to us by another attorney because the attorney could not settle the case and the case was headed to trial. Knee injuries in automobile collision cases have a higher success rate in settlement compared to other injuries. That's because, unlike the complicated issues related to back injuries, most people don't walk around with knee injuries. A torn meniscus, a torn ACL, a torn MCL, or any of the most common disorders of the knees are often, albeit not always, caused traumatically and require immediate care.

Well, in our case, we had a healthy mortgage broker who was on his way to his boss' house. It was the night of the big company holiday party. Unfortunately for this broker and his wife, their vehicle was hit by the bed of a tow truck. Fortunately for them, their son was not in the car. The bed of the tow truck intruded all the way into their backseat and came within inches of our client's head. The only injury he suffered in the accident was torn cartilage in one knee. You would think that everybody would think as my client did: he was lucky.

In the medical records it was noted that my client refused to get immediate surgery. He also did not go to his physical therapy visits consistently. He also did not visit his doctor and missed appointments because he was hopeful, as were his doctors, that his knee pain was not torn cartilage but just a sprain. After a few weeks of therapy, he actually tried to go golfing. Unfortunately, he only made it about three holes into golfing and realized he simply could not continue to put weight on his leg.

He mentioned to one of his doctors, just prior to being sent to surgery that he had tried to golf but was unable to finish. That makes sense doesn't it? The man who tore cartilage in his knee a few weeks earlier probably is not going to be able to finish golfing.

Now, we think that he should be applauded. He didn't just sit around going from doctor to doctor jumping into surgery. He tried to do whatever he could do, tough it out, and hoped he would get better. The waiting failed to help and it turned out he had to have the surgery.

What do you think the insurance company did with that medical record? Believe it or not, we ended up trying that case because the insurance company hired a doctor who was willing to testify that our client must have injured his knee golfing! That's right, even though the medical records well documented the fact that he had injured his knee on the night of the collision, even though he had never had knee pain or problems prior to this incident, and even though he was in therapy at the time, the insurance company's doctor took the position that, in fact, he must've hurt his knee golfing.

Did the insurance company win? No! We ended up getting a verdict that was for more money than we asked for at the time of trial. It was a fair result and it was, at least in our view, a ridiculous defense.

We've seen single missed appointments turn into blown up charts by insurance company lawyers to show that our client could not have been hurt. How could missing an appointment or two with the doctor prove somebody wasn't hurt? Because, apparently in the world that some people live in, life never gets too hectic or unexpectedly busy. The argument made by these companies is that somebody who misses a doctor's appointment must not really be hurt, because if they were hurt they would not miss the doctor's appointment in the first place.

Don't laugh at how silly it is for a defense lawyer to suggest that doctor's appointments should never be missed. These arguments are repeatedly made to avoid a fair settlement. The bottom line is when someone is an injury victim, they must make sure their doctor visits are consistent. An injury victim should also follow the advice of their doctor and follow up on referrals, or risk something less than a fair resolution to the claim. Even if it happens that the injured person has to cancel an appointment or two, they should make sure there are not significant gaps in time during the course of their medical treatment. They should ensure that they tell their treating doctors and medical providers the ways that the injury is affecting their life. In doing these things, it will help avoid spending much more time fighting for the justice that is deserved.

MISTAKE #7

ASSUMING LOST WAGES AUTOMATICALLY WILL BE PAID

An injury victim must prove the amount of money he/she lost from work as a result of the injury. We know this may sound simple, but it can create significant challenges if not documented adequately. Even when a personal injury victim knows what hurdles they face to recover their lost wages, some victim's circumstances still present significant challenges to obtaining the full reimbursement of the wages they lost.

1) Obtaining Medical Documentation: A Doctor's Note

Yes, we know this sounds like you are in elementary school; however, every insurance company will request a note from a doctor that says the person is unable to work. The note can be a simple note. It can even be on a script that the doctor usually hands out for prescriptions. This note is best when it includes information such as the specific limitation that prevents work, the specific fact that someone cannot work, and the date the injury victim will be able to return to work. Once the date to return to work arrives, the injured person that is unable to return to work must get a new slip. Every case is different but this is general information for documenting lost wages.

Unless the injured person is in a coma, or is in in-patient care at a hospital or rehabilitation facility, a detailed doctor's note is usually needed to decrease the likelihood of an argument over why the person was unable to return to work at that time. Sometimes, it is even helpful to have both the family doctor and the specialist doctor write the note to even further document the inability to work. Why is it necessary to get not one, but two different "permission slips" documenting the physical limitations? Because it is possible to attack the opinion of a single doctor, but it is much harder to do when two unaffiliated doctors came to the same conclusion at the time of the incident.

2) Getting documentation from the employer

The fact that a doctor says an injured person cannot work is not enough to prove loss of wages actually occurred because of the injury. To do this, it is vital to obtain documentation from the employer showing the work history of the person, how much they had made prior to the incident, and how much money was not paid out following the injury.

It is even worth documenting the lost time from work that was paid through paid sick time and vacation time. This leave time was lost as a result of the negligence of someone else, and you are entitled to be reimbursed for that loss, just as you are entitled to the money you lost in wages that would have been earned. Some employers will provide all of the documentation needed, such as describing the injured person's job responsibilities, positions, how long that person has been employed prior to the incident, and so forth.

Like almost every claim being made by the seriously injured, there are hurdles put in their path to recover wages that will be lost in the future as a result of the incident. What about the commissioned salesperson whose income changes significantly over time? What about the commissioned salesperson who changes jobs once a year and therefore has no real pattern of income? What of the business owner and entrepreneur who has just started building his business and therefore has very little in the way of profits thus far?

Of course, maybe the worst thing to see, what about the waiters, waitresses and other workers who make money in tips, and let's face it, rarely report everything that they have made when it comes to income tax time.

LOST FUTURE EARNINGS, A.K.A. DIMINISHED CAPACITY

If all of those challenges to actual lost earnings sounds difficult to prove, what about the decreased ability to earn future income? Remember, the settlements and verdicts are a one-time event. There is no chance to return later to get money when someone is unable to do their job after five years as they would have been if not for the incident. Thus, many times we have to prove that there will be a future wage loss and set out to obtain the necessary evidence. In addition to the inherent challenge of proving something that is not going to take place until the future, there are other challenges, as well.

What of the landscaper who is 32 years old and is now walking with a limp. How long will he be able to be a landscaper? In other words, in a system that requires the plaintiff be allowed only one chance at recovery, and yet requires the plaintiff to carry the burden of proof as to how much is going to be lost, how can that person possibly prove how much will be lost in the future (perhaps over the next three decades) just two years after the injury?

There are expert witnesses that can be hired who are good at projecting lost future income. There are economists and vocational rehabilitation experts who can help out in this regard. Proving lost wages and future lost wages can be very tricky. There is no absolute answer to some of these questions, especially for those who can return to work somewhere, but cannot return to work at the job they held prior to the incident as a result of the injuries they suffered. Sometimes, it is even more complicated where the injury does not prevent a return to the same job, but prevents the person from working as many hours as he did prior to the incident.

MISTAKE #8

FAILING TO SAY "NO" TO A REQUEST FOR A RECORDED STATEMENT

"Recorded statements" are commonly requested by insurance companies of the person who brings an injury claim. In other words, after somebody is hurt, you can expect in most cases the insurance company will ask the victim to give a "recorded statement." Ask them, the insurance company, adjusters and employees, why they want a recorded statement and they will tell you quite clearly that it is simply because they "want to know what happened."

Really? We "want to know what happened" all the time. Sometimes we want to know what happened when one kid comes upstairs crying about what another child of ours did to him. (With 7 children this happens often, by the way!) Do you know what we do? We ask what happened. Do you know what we don't do? We do not record the conversation. Sometimes we want to know what happened from a particular client. Do you know what we do? We ask the client what happened. Do you know what we don't do? We don't record the conversation.

It makes sense that the insurance company wants to know what happened. Gathering information and making decisions based upon that information is necessary in what they do. The idea that it has to be recorded raises a whole set of new issues. Are they really recording it just for future documentation? They are certainly not just recording it so that they can "know what happened." We almost never allow our clients to give recorded statements. We doubt it has happened even where our own insurance company has claimed it was a part of the insurance contract and our clients were "required" to give recorded statements. In our office, we fight this nonsense for our clients, preventing the unnecessary intrusion.

The truth is, there is a reason the insurance companies want to record the statement. They want to be able to take the statements given to them, hand them to their lawyers, so the insurance company's lawyer can potentially twist and turn and take some statement out of context. A statement that was usually made while the victim was in pain and discomfort, and likely speaking freely and honestly, but not watching every choice of word carefully.

Would you like an example? How about the beginning of a conversation where the adjuster asks the injured person how they are doing and the person who has been hurt says "I'm doing fine." Now, that may be just a normal response that you get to any question asked in a greeting every day.

"How are you doing?"

"Fine."

Can you imagine when it comes to settlement having to justify how you were "doing fine" when you gave the recorded statement? Meanwhile, at the time these statements are taken the person is sometimes in the hospital and often doped up on narcotic pain prescriptions to lessen the pain they are experiencing. Yet this is the type of nonsense that a simple, well-meaning, honest victim can often encounter just by simply allowing a statement to be recorded. This is typical of the kind of apparently harmless requests that are made by the insurance company with particularly harmful consequences.

Are the harmful consequences of these statements taken with the purpose of denying justice to the victim? We are sure that most insurance company adjusters and employees would argue that the reason they are recording the statement is to make sure no one can later claim that they took statements down incorrectly or that they missed important statements of fact. We're sure they want to avoid any allegations of impropriety and a recorded statement does document each word that was stated at that time.

However, having seen these statements twisted and turned and abused down the road, used as excuses repeatedly (by those clients we have taken on after the time they have given the recorded statement but before they became our clients) we can tell you that the reality of it is that a recorded statement later is used for purposes other than just getting to the truth of the matter. Unfortunately, many of our clients come to us after they have already given a recorded statement. We can usually overcome the anticipated twisting of words by the adverse party from what was stated in the recorded statement. Still, getting a favorable result is more likely when these recorded statements are not provided.

MISTAKE #9

FILLING OUT INSURANCE FORMS AND QUESTIONNAIRES

Just like recorded statements, the same can be said of the "forms" that insurance companies will demand people fill out. We will often see these forms that have either been filled out by people before they retained our office, or provided to our client before we were able to notify the insurance company that we had been retained in a particular case. These forms are filled with broad questions intended to elicit the most rambling possible response by a well-intentioned and honest injury victim so that these statements can later be used against that same person.

Perhaps you're saying to yourself at this point "but I would tell the truth." Or maybe "simply tell the truth." If it were only that simple, forms and recorded statements would not be used as a weapon on repeated occasions.

Of course, the victim is required to tell the truth. Of course, anyone should be punished if they lie about what happened. Of course, of course, of course. Now, let's get past that simple reality and accept the fact that there is a person on the other side, somebody who has a job to do. That job is not to find the truth, but to put their side- the defense, the side against you - in the best possible position.

Most people tell the truth. But don't you agree that the truth can be twisted and turned by an adversary who is not looking to get to the truth of the matter, but is looking to put a spin on things? It absolutely, positively can be in some situations. It is not a risk worth taking. Have you ever seen on TV (or maybe in real life) the reading of the "Miranda warnings" by the police to a criminal suspect? You know the one, "anything you say can and will be used against you in a court of law."

Before we became lawyers, we had trouble with the Miranda warnings. Maybe it was over thinking, but we could not agree with the statements necessarily being used against the person.

People think statements can be used against them only if they lie, but with a personal injury claim that's simply not true. We can tell you that in many cases, written or recorded statements obtained by the insurance company "can" and "will be" used against you. It doesn't matter that the person was telling the truth. It is not enough that the victim was being completely honest. It's being requested to be filled out for a particular purpose in mind and that is to minimize the amount of the settlement.

Is it evil in any way for the insurance company to request forms about your injuries be filled out? Is there something wrong with the fact that they simply are gathering the facts with forms that they are sending to someone? In theory, absolutely not. The insurance industry is required to make a factual inquiry into every claim made against them. How could they possibly proceed if they didn't do this? The problem is not in the theory.

The problem is in the application of that theory and the fact that these companies are allowed to use these basic procedures to later twist and turn against the people who are well intentioned. It is, in reality, one-sided. The resources of the insurance company, combined with their position of being the one that is called by the injured party, allows them to get information from willing injured victims who don't understand the legal arena. In contrast, relatively few defendants ever provide recorded statements to lawyers like ourselves. In practice, it is one more advantage the insurance companies and big business possess in fighting these claims.

You may be sitting there right now saying to yourself that it is unfair to blame the insurance company for the statements made by these injury victims. Here's the reality: people who are trying to "game the system" or who try to lie or steal or manipulate the process would almost never give statements like these. The people who give the statements are exactly the kind of people – the honest people with integrity – that later have the statement twisted, taken out of context, or in other ways used against them.

MISTAKE #10

MISSING THE STATUTE OF LIMITATIONS BLINDLY TRUSTING THE ADVERSARY – A RECIPE FOR DISASTER

When we had just started our practice, literally weeks into the practice, a man walked into our office. He came into our office because he had missed the "statute of limitations." The statute of limitations is a time limit on every personal injury action. It is a tool to force plaintiffs to either settle their case or file a lawsuit by a certain date. The goal is a necessary one, to prevent someone from suing a defendant 25 years after a crash that should have been handled within 2 years of the crash. The limitations allows the defendants to move forward without worrying that they will be sued many years later, and increases the likelihood that witnesses and evidence will still be available.

This young man had been talking with the insurance company since the days following the day he was rear-ended by their insured. He was required to either settle the claim or file a lawsuit with the courts within two years as his case statute of limitations was two years. He thought he had "filed" his claim when he told the insurance company about it. Maybe he should have known better, but this is a common misconception.

In this case, he did not fail to file by the statute of limitations solely out of his own ignorance of the law. He had a lot of "help" missing the time deadline, and that help came from the insurance company that would benefit from his failure.

For the two years following the date of the collision, the insurance adjuster repeatedly told this young man that he should not try to settle this case until he was done with all of his treatment. So, this claimant who had a permanent, jaw injury as a result of the collision continued to seek intermittent treatment from an oral surgeon. That treatment lasted just over two years.

Unbeknownst to this man, the statute of limitations in Arizona is two years and it does not just mean telling the insurance company about a claim, but filing a lawsuit with an Arizona Court. He found out, too late, that the claim with the insurance company does not give an injury victim any legal rights in that setting. Instead, it is necessary to file a lawsuit or have the case settled in two years or all rights are lost.

Nobody would take this man's case. We were young lawyers with a new practice and decided to take on the fight for him. We knew it was going to be a long battle to prove the insurance company "tricked him" into missing the statute of limitations. During the "discovery" portion of the case – where we collect evidence to try to prove our case before trial – we were able to get evidence that the insurance adjuster had repeatedly told our client that he must wait to settle his case until he is done with treatment.

After being released from the doctor, our client immediately went into the insurance company office to finally get his medical bills paid. Turns out, this little trip came two years and one week after his collision, one week after the statute of limitations had run.

The employees of the insurance company literally laughed at him. They mocked him. They belittled him because he had trusted them and thus missed the statute of limitations. As you might imagine, the insurance company did not want to pay a penny on a case where the statute of limitations had run. This turned into a hard-fought case that went all the way to trial before we were able to get a recovery for this client.

The worst part is that it all could have been avoided. It would have been avoided if this man had simply remembered that everybody has a role. Even a friendly and well meaning adjuster could leave you in a difficult position that destroys your case. The adjuster might not even realize that as the injured victim, you are relying on what he is saying each time you speak. Relying on the words of an adjuster ultimately can bring horrific results because an adjuster is not acting in your best interest. And, of course, without special training, experience or knowledge, how can a victim even know whether they are being dealt with honestly or what statutes they need to meet and how the statute of limitations work?

They can't.

Again, there is something of a theme here. It is often the most honest, the well-intentioned, the least "greedy" of people that are actually taken advantage of in this legal system. Because of their failure to be on the lookout for others who are misleading them (sometimes intentionally and sometimes unintentionally) or not looking out for them, they get caught up in situations and their rights are jeopardized.

THE STATUTE OF LIMITATIONS: WHAT YOU DON'T KNOW CAN HURT YOU

Almost every kind of action that can be brought has a time deadline which prevents somebody from bringing that claim after a certain period of time. For instance, where we practice in Arizona, a business can sue another business for a breach of contract six years after the fact. The statute of limitations is a great idea, in that it prevents someone from suing you for something that happened 25 years ago. Not only does it just seem inherently unfair to be sued for something that happened 25 years ago, it's also true that witnesses and evidence and other things get lost over time. Memories fade over time. There has to be some limitation in the amount of time that someone can bring an action.

But again, how long should that limitation be? If one business can sue another business for six years after the fact, if that's a fair amount of time that a breach of contract claim can be made, why is an injury claim sometimes limited to as little as 180 days?

In Arizona, for instance, if the proper paperwork is not filed against a negligent governmental entity within 180 days, the claim is lost. Understand here, we're not just talking about disputed cases. Even where the government admits it is at fault, the proper paperwork must be filed in less than six months. Even where everybody agrees the injury was severe, or even where the government admits it caused the death of an innocent person through its own neglect, the proper paperwork must be filed in less than six months.

Do you think most people who lose a loved one are calling a lawyer in under six months? No. Not if they don't know about this law or if nobody encourages them to make an immediate phone call. How about somebody who is severely injured, do you really think most people immediately think about calling a lawyer? Even if they do think about it, do they really take action that quickly?

We can tell you that we get phone calls on a regular basis from people who would have had every right to bring a claim, but simply did not contact a lawyer quickly enough so they missed the statute of limitations.

The reality is that a statute of limitations of only two years or less simply works to the benefit of the defendants, and against the average person who becomes a victim of another's reckless actions. There are just a large number of people that never have the opportunity to bring their claim because they did not know they had to get a lawyer that quickly. This is particularly a disadvantage to the severely injured. Perhaps somebody who just has a whiplash injury that heals in two or three months will have plenty of time to get a lawyer within two years, but what about the person who spends a year and a half under significant and constant medical care. Is that person at fault for not seeking out a lawyer earlier in the game?

Understand that two years does not really mean two years. If most people walk into a lawyer's office one month before the statute of limitations is going to run on a serious injury case, they may not be able to hire a lawyer who is willing to accept the risk of getting the lawsuit filed in time so close to the time limit. There's just too many "i's" to be dotted and "t's" to be crossed in that little of time for many lawyers to be willing to risk accepting a case at that point.

Should the statute of limitations be extended to something closer to the six-year period for negligence claims? In particular, if the only money being sought is from an insurance company that sold a policy to cover somebody for a loss, should the statute of limitations allow the lawsuit to be brought against the insurance company's policy for more than two years?

Of course, this is a public policy decision. But the reality is that this short statute of limitations time frame is simply one more benefit to the insurance companies.

Remember, filing a claim with the insurance company is not the same as filing a lawsuit. If you have not filed a lawsuit within the statute of limitations, you will lose your right to bring a claim. Also, we have discussed only a limited amount of the large number of statute of limitations. Statute of limitation periods vary for filing against your own insurance company, for dog bites, and for many other claims. Statutes of limitations must be considered and applied on a case by case basis. What is vital is that you understand that there are statute of limitations which require you to file an actual lawsuit in an Arizona Court to preserve your case. Knowing what the time period is for your case is something you should ask a lawyer.

MISTAKE #11

NOT BEING AWARE OF LIENHOLDERS PRIOR TO SETTLEMENT

Medical and Other Provider Liens: Making sure the Victims gets compensated

"Liens" are another part of a personal injury claim which can be very complex. There are many types of liens that can "attach" to a personal injury claim. A lien may come from many different entities and in many different forms. The laws relating to liens and personal injury claims is ever-changing, widely-varying, and particularly complex. For our purposes here, suffice to say that a lien in a personal injury setting is a claim by somebody other than the victim that they are entitled to a portion of the final settlement.

The most common type of lien is a medical lien, where a doctor or hospital claims that they are owed money out of a settlement. Again, this takes too many forms to discuss in this setting. Also, some liens are consensual while others are contested. There are some doctors who, for a variety of reasons, are willing to treat a person who has no insurance but needs medical care, as long as the injured party agrees to pay the doctor when a settlement is received. This type of lien is rarely contested because in most cases where this type of lien exists the doctor provided an excellent service to the client for the promise to be paid at a later date. We work with many doctors that offer this service.

On the other hand, there are some liens that are hotly contested. Sometimes, a lien holder – doctor or hospital, for instance – will demand extra payment from someone even though they have already been paid by the person themselves or the health insurance, claiming they should receive more money than they normally would have simply because the treatment they provided was injury-related.

There are times where this leads to disputes over whose names should be on the settlement check, the terms of the settlement, or worse: in some cases there are new lawsuits that spring forth after the original lawsuit is settled.

A trap for the unwary is what liens can turn into. Someone representing themselves, or someone without an experienced personal injury lawyer, can sometimes finish a case thinking they have obtained a certain amount of compensation, only to watch most or all of the money get paid to someone who may not even be deserving of additional payments. Knowing how to fight the inappropriate lien claims has become a vital part of personal injury practice.

There are many types of potential lien holders waiting to get a portion of the injured victim's settlement money, One such type of lien we have in Arizona is called a "balance billing" lien. The law allows a hospital, among others, to get paid not just from a victim's health insurance company but also to pursue extra money from the victim's settlement.

For instance, for those of us who have health insurance, when we go to the hospital we know the hospital may bill $5,000.00 for that treatment, but the hospital may only be reimbursed $2,500.00 from our health insurance company. Do we owe the other $2,500.00? Of course, not. That is the deal that is made between our health insurance company and the medical provider.

However, the "powers that be" have decided that even though a hospital cannot come after you for the difference in most cases, if you are going to be given money for pain, suffering, anxiety, loss of enjoyment of life, and other things that you have personally suffered, the hospital gets to make a greater profit from your settlement. The one caveat is that the law says the medical provider must follow the specific language of the statute for the lien to be valid.

If the law on balance billing is not followed correctly, no lien exists under the law. Moreover, there are certain types of claims that cannot be "liened" under this law. Knowing these details and where the fight can be won can be a key component to getting a reasonable settlement actually to the deserving person, the victim, as opposed to the settlement going to increase hospital profits.

There are many hidden "liens" like this that most people never know about until they disburse the proceeds of the settlement and get a call – sometimes even two years after the settlement! There are also other liens that need to be addressed in an injury claim, including Medicare liens, health insurance liens, and doctor's liens, which may exist even when they have accepted your health insurance.

If you have sustained a serious injury and have significant medical bills, it is vital that all these potential liens be addressed prior to settlement. If some health insurance adjuster or doctor notified you 2 months after the settlement and said they expected $50,000 out of your settlement, that could be financially devastating.

We should tell you this is one area where an experienced attorney can make a huge impact. An experienced attorney will fight whether the lien is valid, at all. If the lien is determined to be valid, an experienced attorney should be able to work with the lien holder to have them reduce their lien amount in the majority of cases. Let's face it, the job of the lawyer is not to just get a fair settlement, but to make sure that fair settlement makes it to the injury victim.

MISTAKE # 12

FAILING TO CONSULT WITH A LAWYER

In most situations, the best way to decide whether you need to hire a lawyer is to talk to a lawyer about the case. The more information you have prior to discussing your claim with a lawyer, the better chance you have to make an informed decision and ask the questions you need answered. A good place to start is to understand the earlier chapter that discusses whether a personal injury case even exists.

As you would expect, we speak to people almost every day that are trying to decide if they need a lawyer to help them on their potential personal injury case. In our practice, we often tell people requesting a lawyer that they do not need an attorney.

For example, if someone was involved in a "fender bender," that person probably does not need an attorney. If someone went to a single doctor's visit after a motorcycle crash, that person probably does not need the help of an attorney, either. While the people in these scenarios have personal injury claims, their injuries were fortunately minimal.

To hire a lawyer in a case where someone returns to complete health immediately is usually a waste of time and effort, in our view. A good personal injury lawyer is most important and vital to the claim when the outcome of the case can have dramatic effects on the injured person's life. For those lucky enough to avoid injury, the need to get a lawyer usually does not exist.

An attorney is necessary when someone is involved in an incident where they have suffered a serious injury that has affected their ability to participate in their normal activities of daily living. An injury victim who will have a permanent injury should most definitely consult with a lawyer.

If the medical bills are too large to pay, the lost wages are too much to handle, or the expenses are piling up and affecting someone's life, that person needs discuss the situation with an experienced lawyer. Of course, any family that has lost a loved one due to another's neglect, and thus has a potential wrongful death claim, should always discuss the matter with a qualified lawyer. An injury victim who does not consult an attorney on such cases virtually assures herself that she will not achieve a fair settlement.

AT WHAT POINT SHOULD ONE LOOK FOR AN EXPERIENCED PERSONAL INJURY LAWYER

An injury victim should consult an attorney as soon as possible. Deciding whether to consult with a lawyer, at all, can often be a difficult decision. Some people take many months to approach an attorney and this is often a mistake. Some cases require work by an attorney almost immediately due to evidence that must be preserved or statements that must be taken as we have already discussed in earlier chapters. Also, as you have already learned, there are time deadlines that limit the ability to recover in any given case, and the risk of allowing those time deadlines to pass accidentally is too great to prolong making the decision to speak with an attorney.

Many of the self-representation mistakes can be made at the outset of a case, which means just the delay in hiring a lawyer can have devastating effects. We understand that most people want to "do the right thing." We understand that there is a normal, natural concern about getting a lawyer, hiring the right lawyer, and whether to avoid lawyers altogether. That being said, if you have an ongoing injury claim and have waited to consult an attorney until after reading this book, you will be armed with more knowledge about the process of pursuing a personal injury claim and should be better able to choose the attorney that is right for you.

TO HIRE OR NOT HIRE A LAWYER, THAT IS THE QUESTION

OK, let us be clear here: We are biased. We are personal injury lawyers.

People ask us this all of the time. The law can be complicated. Trying to figure out the best way to handle your case, without the help of a good lawyer, can have devastating consequences. For all of the pointers we can share in this book, it is just a fraction of the information one needs to know to appropriately handle a personal injury claim. It would take far more than one book to adequately convey all of the pitfalls and traps for the unwary.

Sometimes it appears that there is not adequate insurance coverage following an injury, but a good lawyer can uncover policies or assets that the defendant may have that can help compensate you for your losses. Other times, it may be that you have failed to recognize a proper defendant who should be pursued in a more complicated case. Trying to handle your own case is usually a mistake. At a minimum, speaking to a lawyer who is knowledgeable is the right decision in any potential serious injury case.

It is our opinion that in a situation where there is a serious personal injury or wrongful death case, it is better in almost every situation to get a lawyer. We hate to use the analogy we have heard many lawyers make comparing handling a personal injury case without a lawyer to operating on yourself. The fact is that, unless you are much tougher than most people, you are incapable of being your own surgeon and operating on yourself.

It is, therefore, obvious to everyone that they cannot be their own surgeon, whether they want to or not. On the other hand, people can be their own lawyer, which means they are fully capable of handling their case and proceeding to destroy it themselves! (As an aside, we are aware of one local surgeon who claims he performed his own vasectomy, claiming there were certain things he just couldn't trust anyone else to do!)

Sometimes pursuing an honest, straightforward assessment is just as valuable to someone's conscience as anything else they may do. Get the answers, gather the information, then make a decision. It is one thing to choose not to hire a lawyer after speaking with an expert in the area. That is an informed decision. Failing to even gather the information and speak to a lawyer? In our view, that is a decision based on ignorance, made at the victim's own peril.

Even if everything else was equal, sometimes it is the threat of a possible lawsuit that can carry as much weight as anything. If the adverse party does not think you are willing to file a lawsuit, they may be less likely to try to resolve the case on fair terms. They have less incentive to offer a fair settlement if they think you will "go away" and settle no matter what they offer. Just having a lawyer is often a signal that you are willing to protect your rights if a fair offer is not made. That, alone, can make discussing your case with an attorney worthwhile. Since all cases do not require an attorney, if you consult with a reputable attorney they should be able to advise you as to how an attorney can help on your case, and if the attorney is not needed, they should at least be able to give you valuable pointers in the best way to handle your claim to its conclusion.

INSURANCE ADJUSTERS HAVE A JOB TO DO

Insurance adjusters have a job to do, and that job does not include being your friend. The adverse insurance adjuster is not on your side. An experienced insurance adjuster is well-versed in the law and armed with the information that favors his or her side of the argument. What kind of person works for insurance companies? What type of individual agrees to be a part of this often vilified industry? The same neighbors, friends, and family members that we all know, like, and trust on most days. Are there greedy insurance company employees who will destroy evidence, lie, and cheat to deny someone insurance benefits? Yes.

Is this the norm? Of course, not.

We have personally been involved in cases where we were convinced that certain insurance company employees, or certain insurance companies, were doing things that were against the insurance industry policies. We have known adjusters to lie. Do these exceptions justify the near-hatred some people have for the entire insurance industry? We don't think so.

However, the fact remains that insurance adjusters have a job to do. It is their job to pay as little as possible to the innocent injury victim. That is part of why it is important to have someone on your side whose job it is to obtain a fair settlement for you, and keep the insurance company honest. An injury victim needs an attorney on their side to protect their rights and make sure they are made "whole." On a case where the victim was lucky enough to not suffer serious injury, the difference between being fairly compensated and taken advantage of may not have a huge effect on the victim's life. When a more serious injury is involved, however, it can make a massive difference on the rest of the injured person's life.

The insurance industry is part of the fabric that makes our society work. If you took the insurance industry out of the United States, we could not function as we currently do, either economically or as a society. We rely upon and trust insurance companies to be there in case of a disaster. Can you imagine a world where one single fire could not only destroy your personal and irreplaceable belongings, but could leave you bankrupt? Were it not for insurance, one fire to company headquarters could destroy even a thriving business. You must remember the job of an insurance company is to make sure they protect the profits for their shareholders. They are, as we are in our practice and almost every business in this country formed to be, a for-profit enterprise. They not only have the right to try to make profits, they have an obligation to attempt to profit from their business.

There is nothing inherently evil about insurance companies, but injury victims have to remember that in evaluating claims, the insurance adjuster's job is to help the insurance company make a profit, although the insurance industry will not say it in quite those terms. Nonetheless, we all understand that the insurance company is trying to achieve profits, and if it can do so at someone's expense, so be it.

In fact, some of the major insurance companies keep statistics on their settlements. Some documents that were obtained from one of the major insurance companies in the United

States revealed that injury victims that hired attorneys obtained a settlement nearly 2-3 times higher than the settlements received by claimants that did not hire an attorney.

MISTAKE #13

FAILING TO CHOOSE THE RIGHT LAWYER

Every State has different requirements pertaining to its lawyers. If you are outside of Arizona, it is important to note that some of these criteria might not apply in your State. Anywhere in the United States, however, most of these questions are worth asking before you hire an attorney and are important to your representation. When you go to hire an attorney ask them the following questions:

1. Are you a Certified Specialist in Injury & Wrongful Death Law?

A "State Bar" governs almost every state - if not every single state - in the country when it comes to who may be a lawyer. This is why only a lawyer can represent you. To become a lawyer, most states require the individual to have graduated from a university with a minimum of a 4-year degree, followed by what is usually an additional 3 years at an accredited law school. Even that is not enough, as every lawyer must pass an exam that goes 2-3 days, depending on the state, in order to become a lawyer in that state.

Lawyers are allowed to practice any area of the law whether they have experience or additional training in that area or not. While a pediatrician is not allowed to do heart transplants, and a neurologist does not treat people for lung infections, any lawyer can accept a personal injury claim at any time. This does not make the person an expert, and does not even mean they have the training to properly handle the case.

Presumably to help the average person identify those lawyers who had the requisite training, the State Bar in many states, including Arizona, certifies a limited number of attorneys as "specialists" in Injury & Wrongful Death Law. This certification is only given out to lawyers who have passed an exam, received the requisite recommendations and approval from Judges and other attorneys, and those who have also shown that they have significant trial experience.

Many lawyers will take personal injury cases, but this is not their area of expertise. By hiring a certified specialist, you will know that you are picking an attorney who has a significant amount of experience and has already been judged by his or her peers in the community as meeting this high standard. Of course, there are attorneys who are not certified specialists who can do a good job on your case; however, by hiring a certified specialist you are more likely to receive the representation and client service that is needed when you have been injured by someone else's negligence.

Currently, less than 2% of all Arizona lawyers have been certified as specialists in Injury and Wrongful Death. Thus, the "recommendation" that one friend gives to another is not likely to be to someone who has earned this distinction from the State Bar, and finding out if you are entrusting a case to someone that is truly qualified is vital.

2. Is your practice mostly personal injury law?

Many attorneys handle "a few" personal injury cases. When you interview an attorney, it is important to ask the attorney what type of law they practice. If an attorney practices just personal injury, they are probably more likely to know what they are doing and more likely to achieve a fair and reasonable settlement. There are changes in every area of the law on a regular basis. Just attempting to stay ahead of all of these changes in one area of the law is a challenge. If an attorney handles cases in multiple areas of the law, it is more likely that they do not have the experience and knowledge that is necessary to handle a serious injury case and achieve a successful result.

3. Will my case matter to your office or will I be just another number?

When you have been seriously injured, you want to know your case is important to the lawyers in the firm. Talk to the attorney and make sure that they will be able to give you the attention you deserve. It is important to know that you and your case will not just be "another number." There are some firms that take as many cases as they can without paying attention to the individual clients and their unique needs and goals. Personal injury is not a "one size fits all" type of law. It is about people, not just about the paperwork that is part of this area of law. It is important to get a feel for the attorney and firm you retain and make sure you have a "gut feeling" that tells you that you are more than just another number.

4. What is your experience (years in practice)?

There are some attorneys who are just starting out who will be able to do a fantastic job for you. Many attorneys who are only recently admitted to the bar and just recently out of law school are bold enough to start their own office. (We did!) If you pick an attorney who is just starting out or an attorney who does not focus their practice on personal injury, you need to take extra precautions and ask more questions until you feel comfortable that they know what they are doing, and have the competence to achieve the best possible results.

When we started out, we often asked questions to more experienced attorneys. We were not shy about asking questions. We also had the benefit of having worked at other firms and for other lawyers. However, our "full steam ahead" approach is probably not the norm. We are proud of the representation we provided in those early years. Having said that, we also knew which cases we could handle and in which cases we would need to consult with more experienced lawyers. Experience is not everything. A great lawyer is not always the most experienced lawyer. However, experience has its benefits, and this is a worthwhile question that needs to be asked.

5. Do you take cases to trial?

Some attorneys want to settle cases, never go to the courthouse and try a case. One way an attorney can ensure that the defense will pay the full amount owed on a case is due to the threat of taking the case to trial. The insurance industry has all of the information it can collect inputted into computer programs. Thus, knowing if your attorney tries cases often - or if the attorney has not tried a case in years - is vital. If the attorney never goes to court, the insurance company will know that. They will thus know that, in the end, they can simply wait the case out for as long as it takes to settle the case.

The "threat" of taking the case all the way through the process, to the jury, significantly increases the likelihood of a fair result. If you hire a certified specialist, they already have shown that they have significant trial experience. Otherwise, they would not have been able to become a certified specialist as trial experience is a requisite part of earning the certified specialist certification.

6. What is your reputation in the legal community?

It is important that the attorney you hire has a solid reputation in the community. You can figure this out in a variety of ways. Remember, the adjusters know the attorneys in your community. They know who will try cases and who will settle. They know what juries will think of attorneys and what attorneys are more likely to prevail. You should ask the attorney if they get cases by referral. If the attorney advertises, do they do so in a professional manner, or do they come across as snake-oil salesmen?

If you are picking an attorney who has a grizzly bear as their firm mascot or proclaims that they offer discount fees in their ad, you may want to consider whether you think this is the type of firm that has built a reputation that allows them to be selective in the cases they take, and whether it seems they have a good reputation in the community. There may be some firms where they discount their fees and do just as good a job as the certified specialist who charges 5% more, but does that sound likely to you? Look for your lawyer with a critical eye, your choice of lawyer is a critical decision.

7. Will you represent me on a contingent fee basis?

Most injury victims - in fact most people in our great country, injured or healthy - cannot afford to pay an attorney by the hour. Ask the attorney if they will represent you on a contingent fee basis. A contingent fee will allow the attorney to take a percentage of the total settlement and you will not have to pay anything up front. The lawyers earn their fee when the case is won by settlement or by a jury verdict.

Ask the attorney if you will be personally responsible for attorneys' fees if, for any reason, the case is not won. Many firms vary greatly in terms of their fee agreement and pursuit of costs from their clients. We are very proud of the fact that every dollar we have earned has come from a victory we have achieved in some form. We have never had a client pay us a single dollar from their own pocket. Every cent of our fees has been earned as a part of the successful conclusion to the case.

8. What happens if I sign up with your firm and change my mind?

Ask the attorney what happens if you sign a fee agreement, but it turns out to not be a good match. You may want to consider whether the lawyer is likely to pursue you for fees if you are not satisfied with the service you have received. The contingency fee agreement should be simple and easy for you to read. Look it over and make sure that there is a clause that specifically says that the lawyer understands the client has the right to cancel the agreement and leave the firm, without some penalty as a result.

9. Do you have malpractice insurance?

In Arizona, attorneys are not required to have malpractice insurance. Anyone can make a mistake, even the best doctor, accountant, lawyer, athlete - you name it. Some mistakes are simply part of the process. Other mistakes fall below the standard of care on a given case. Be sure to ask the lawyer you hire if they carry malpractice insurance, to ensure that if that extremely unlikely mistake occurs on your case due to the negligence of the lawyer, your case is still protected.

10. Ask yourself: Do I feel comfortable with this attorney?

This last one seems obvious, but many times we talk to people years after they had a personal injury case. We have heard on many occasions from people who never felt that they were comfortable with the lawyer they hired. Take the time to pick a lawyer that you feel is a good match for you and your personality, not just your case. It is important that you feel confident about your lawyer and that you are able to be open and honest with the lawyer and law office that you choose. You are going to need to open up and discuss what can sometimes be embarrassing issues with your attorney. It is worth taking the time to ensure that you make this decision only once.

CONCLUSION

This book does not replace the need to consult with and potentially hire an attorney. Hopefully it can help inform and direct you when making the decision if an attorney is needed and how an attorney would be of help. Moreover, we hope you now understand the hurdles that an injured person faces when pursuing their personal injury claim as well as the mistakes that can be made that can destroy your chance to help correct the injustice that was done by a negligent party.

If you have questions or want to see if we are can handle your case you can call us at the numbers below. We are always available to help injured victims as it is our passion. It is our mission to level the playing field between insurance companies and injured victims.

We can be reached by telephone at:
480-753-4534 (East Valley)
602-267-1280 (Central Phoenix)
623-930-8064 (West Valley)
520-624-4428 (Tucson)

We can also be contacted by email:
mark@breyerlaw.com
alexis@breyerlaw.com

WANT A COPY OF OUR NEWSLETTER?

GO TO OUR WEBSITE, **BREYERLAW.COM**, AND FILL OUT THE CONTACT AND MEMO SECTION.

HAVE MORE QUESTIONS?

We can be reached by telephone at:

480-753-4534 (East Valley)

602-267-1280 (Central Phoenix)

623-930-8064 (West Valley)

520-624-4228 (Tucson)